All for Assembly

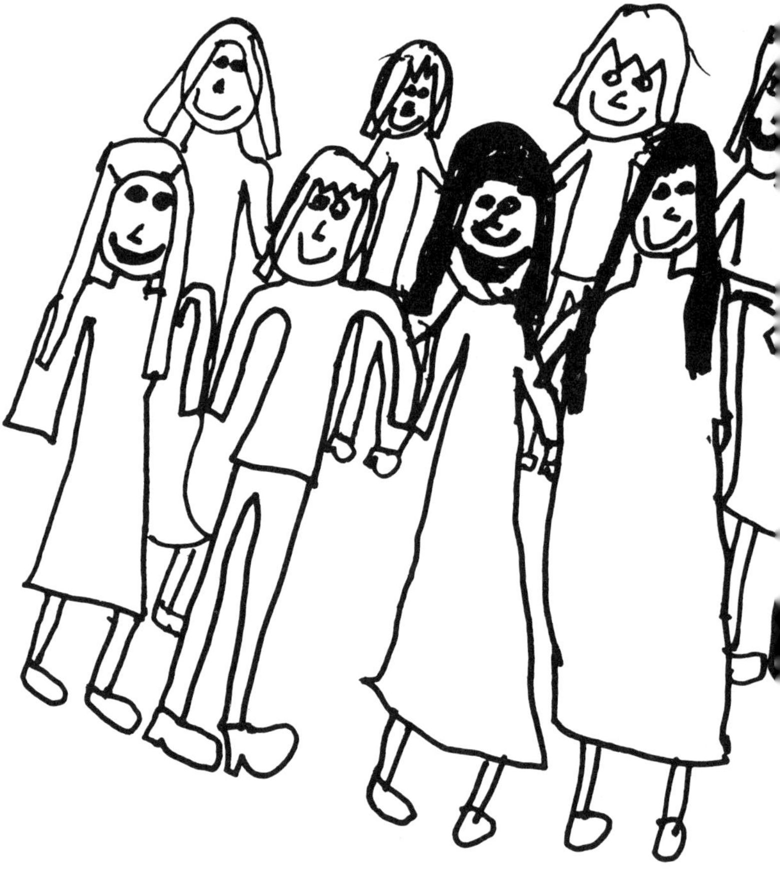

All for Assembly

A resource book for First and Middle Schools

Redvers Brandling

Cambridge University Press
Cambridge
London   New York   New Rochelle
Melbourne   Sydney

Published by the Press Syndicate of the University of Cambridge
The Pitt Building, Trumpington Street, Cambridge CB2 1RP
32 East 57th Street, New York, NY 10022, USA
296 Beaconsfield Parade, Middle Park, Melbourne 3206, Australia

© Cambridge University Press 1983

First published 1983

Printed in Great Britain
at the University Press, Cambridge

ISBN 0 521 28760 X

For permission to reproduce hymns the author and publisher
would like to thank the following:
'Gifts' and 'Shelter the weak' © 1972 High-Fye Music Ltd, 37
Soho Square, London W1V 5DG; 'All the nations' © 1973
Mayhew-McCrimmon Ltd; 'The family of love' and 'The Lord's
my shepherd' © 1973 Josef Weinberger Ltd, reproduced from
Songs of Celebration by permission of the copyright owners;

Prayers: 'Joy' from *Lord of the Morning*, © Lutterworth Press,
1977; 'Optimism' from *Faith, Folk, Festivity* © Stainer & Bell Ltd
and Mayhew McCrimmon; 'Nature' and 'Admiration' ©
National Christian Education Council; 'Forgiveness' from *Prayers
for Young People*, Collins, 1963; 'Everybody' © Stainer & Bell.
The text in 'Easter 1' (A12) appeared originally in *Teacher's
World*, 30 March, 1973.

Cover picture by Lucy Bowden

The majority of the illustrations in the
book are by Lucy Bowden.
Additional illustrations by Susannah Seddon,
and Philip and Mariette Williams.

Contents

Introduction 7
Stories 9
Class Assemblies 55
Music and Assembly 91
Prayers and 'Thoughts' 107
Biblical Material 123
Assemblies and Religions 129
Reminders 139
Resources 151

Acknowledgements

My thanks are due to teachers and pupils, past and present, of St Clement's School and Dewhurst St Mary School, Cheshunt. The unfailing high quality of their assembly presentations has always been a great source of inspiration.

My thanks are also due to Ron Deadman, who, in his years as editor of 'Teachers World' gave me great encouragement whilst writing many articles on assembly. These resulted in numerous contacts with a wide variety of teachers.

It will be seen, as a result of these acknowledgements, that the material contained in this book has been collected over a number of years. Every effort has been made to acknowledge all copyright material, but the publishers would be pleased to hear of any that has been used and not acknowledged.

Introduction

The modern assembly in a primary school is a very different occasion from that envisaged by those educationalists who decreed obligatory collective worship in the 1944 Education Act.

The reasons for this are many. On the one hand there has been increasing secularisation, a decline in the type of Christianity traditionally accepted in 1944, a spread of other religions. On the other hand teachers now seem more concerned that the content of assemblies is relevant and comprehensible to the children involved. Added to this is the availability of more and better books, a wider contact with the skills of presenting, a more flexible approach in schools, better buildings.

Nevertheless, looked at from a teacher's point of view, assemblies are hard taskmasters. The need for stimulating, relevant material is inexhaustible, whilst at the same time there can never be any excuse for an assembly that is less than the best of which the presenters are capable. In their book, *First School RE* (pub. SCM Press), Terence and Gill Copley offer the comment that assemblies must contain 'a sense of expectancy, a willingness to co-operate, some unity between those present by reason of shared experiences or common values.'

No one book could possibly answer all needs for assembly purposes, but it does seem to me that there is a consistent requirement for books that offer practical help, which can be taken up by teachers with special reference to their own school situations.

This book seeks to provide material in a number of areas that are relevant to assembly. I hope it will be used for ideas, suggestions and developments, but an arrangement has also been made which will allow for its use with regard to more 'instant assemblies'.

Key to numbering

The stories in the book have been numbered S1, S2, S3 etc. Class assemblies are numbered A1, A2, A3 etc., prayers P1, P2, P3 etc, and hymns H1, H2, H3 etc.

The significance of this lettering/numbering is made apparent in various sections of the book, but for the user who wishes to choose a 'story, hymn and a prayer' for an assembly, then once a story has been chosen the symbols after it would denote suitable supporting material.

For instance if the story 'Children of Courage' is used then the symbols after it (H5) denote that 'Disciples' would be an appropriate hymn, and that P5, P12, P21 would be useful references for prayers and thoughts.

Stories

This section aims at providing a large variety of concisely told stories and anecdotes that are well suited to the primary school. In my experience almost all stories are better 'told' than read, and presenters of assemblies should have no difficulty in assimilating the material here for 're-telling'.

For those who want a more instant type of assembly, however, the references after each story indicate suitable hymns and prayers to support it (for more details of this see the key to numbering).

The stories themselves are adaptable enough to be used at most times of the year, but for those who want to use them in some sort of pattern, the 'Reminders' section of the book suggests monthly groupings of the stories.

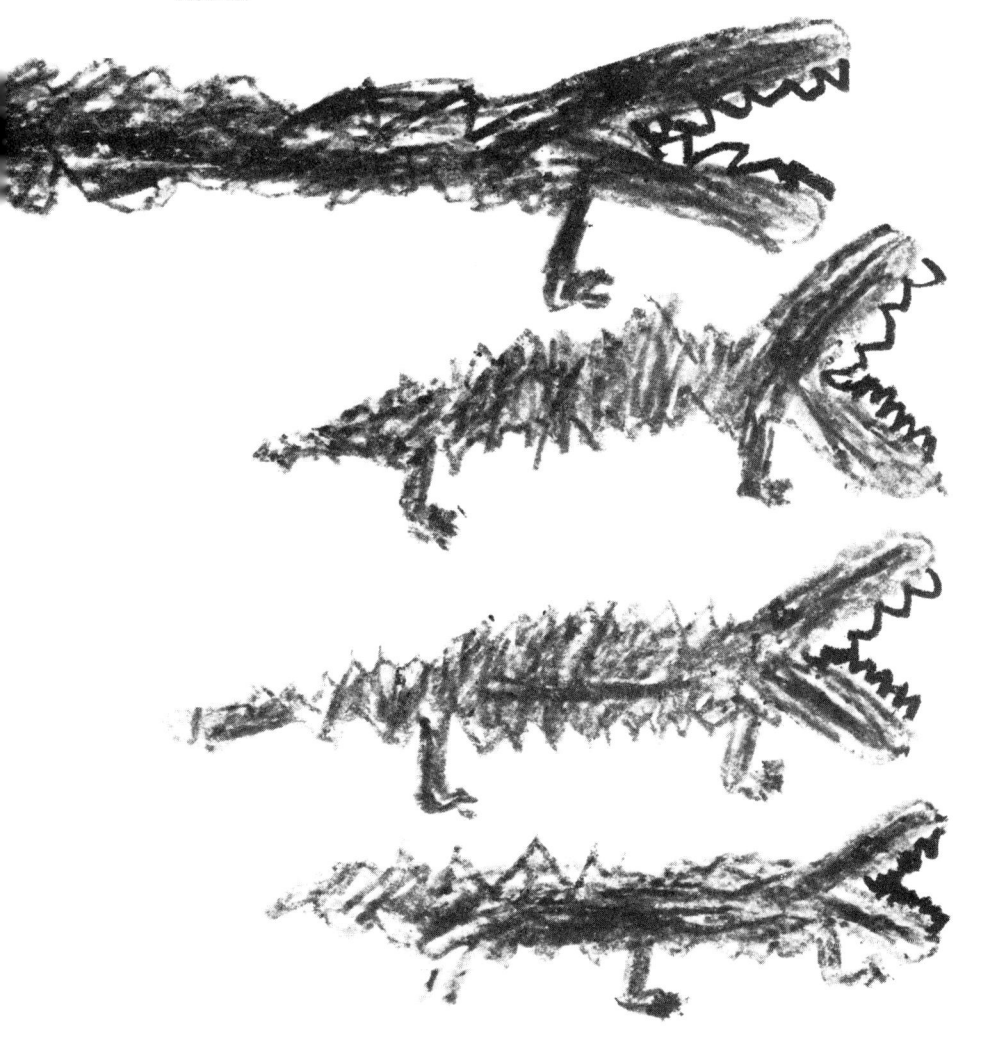

S1 Children of courage

Each year a service is held in Westminster Abbey, during which children who have been outstandingly courageous during the year receive awards. One of the most impressive things about this occasion is the different kinds of courage that the children have shown.

In December 1979 for instance, Princess Alexandra presented an award to five-year-old Charlene Gill, who had shown great determination in overcoming the pain and difficulties caused by having a diseased hip.

Roy Gadd, aged ten, got his award for a very different kind of courage. He and his friend, Kathy Gee, were playing in a field near a circus. Kathy went too near to one of the animals' cages and put her hand through the bars to stroke a leopard. Quickly the leopard seized Kathy's arm in its powerful claws. She was trapped. As soon as Roy saw what had happened he rushed to the cage, punched the leopard on the head and, as its paws eased their grip in surprise, pulled Kathy clear.

Two Vietnamese children received awards for their courage in enduring appalling conditions on a boat in which they were escaping from the troubles of Vietnam. Le Quang Sang, aged twelve, and Le Quan Tuyen, aged ten, were on an overcrowded boat with only a bag of rice between them. When people died they were thrown overboard and their bodies were eaten by sharks. The two boys were finally rescued and, at the time of the award, were being cared for in a Save the Children home in Surrey.

P5, P12, P21

S2 The silent menace

Builders working on a site in Plaistow suddenly came across something very hard where they were digging. After scraping the earth away from the object they suddenly went cold with horror – the thing they had been hitting with their spades was a bomb!

Dropped from a German bomber almost thirty years ago during an air raid on London, the bomb had failed to explode and had lain there ever since. Now, having been disturbed, there was the strong possibility that it would at last explode. Something had to be done urgently.

The first thing was to get everyone nearby to safety. Messages were sent round people's homes and over a thousand people had to leave their houses and flats until the bomb could be made safe. Next, the experts of the army's bomb disposal squad were sent for.

Major Arthur Hogben was the officer made responsible for seeing that the 2,200 lb bomb, already nicknamed 'Hermann', did not go off.

Knowing that everybody was safely out of the way, Major Hogben approached the bomb very carefully. After examining it thoroughly he used steam on the heat-sensitive device to remove nearly a ton of high explosive. When he had finished his extremely dangerous work he knew that the bomb could now never explode. It was then dragged away to be destroyed.

For his courage in risking his life in this calm, thorough way, Major Hogben was awarded the Queen's Gallantry Medal.
H4, P4, P12, P40

S3 The quarrel

The sun shone down on the dry, burning Spanish plain. Pedro, who was riding the horse, mopped his brow with a large red handkerchief.

'All right,' said Alfredo, who was walking beside the horse, 'get down. You've had your hour in the saddle. It's my turn to ride and your turn to walk.'

'Nonsense,' replied Pedro, 'I've got at least another ten minutes yet.'

'You have not!' shouted Alfredo grabbing the horse's reins and bringing it to a stop.

Alfredo then began pulling at Pedro to try and get him off the horse. Meanwhile Pedro hung on desperately to the saddle shouting abuse at Alfredo.

Finally, with a violent heave, Alfredo dragged his companion down into the dust. For a moment or two they lay there scuffling and shouting in the terrific heat. Then, exhausted, they sat up and looked at each other. They then noticed what had happened during their argument. The horse, freed from a rider and frightened by all the commotion, had galloped off and was no longer in sight. Now neither of them could ride.
H3, P15, P19, P42

S4 Saved

It was a cold windy day in Bloomsbury, London. Afternoon shoppers scurried over the windswept pavements, with coat collars turned up and thoughts of warm cups of tea in their minds. Suddenly there was a shout and the bustle of the street came to a standstill.

Sixty feet above the shoppers a man had appeared on a narrow ledge on the roof of one of the houses. Coatless, and with his hair blowing in the wind, he sat on the edge of the parapet with his feet dangling limply. In his arms he held a tiny, crying baby.

The people below were horrified. Obviously the man was ill. One false move and both he and the baby would crash to the street below. A woman made for the nearest telephone kiosk and dialled 999.

Soon the street was a scene of frenzied activity. Several police cars, two ambulances and two fire engines, with escape ladders at the ready, arrived. There was little that they could do, however. Any attempt to get close resulted in warning shouts from the distressed man on the roof. The crowd below began to fear more than ever for both his life and the baby's.

It was then that a twenty-three-year-old woman from a tiny town in Dumbartonshire, Scotland took a hand in events. Policewoman Margaret Cleland had left her native Scotland to work in London because she thought that police work in a city would be interesting. Now, feeling terribly nervous but also very determined, she opened an attic door and stepped out onto the roof. She made no attempt to go near the man but, in a voice as casual as she could make it, began an everyday conversation. The minutes passed dreadfully slowly and soon Margaret had been talking to the man for an hour. As she gained his confidence she edged nearer and nearer to him and the child.

Finally, after almost two hours, she managed to persuade the man that the baby needed a coat to keep it warm. When the man agreed, Margaret held out a coat and as the man took it she seized the baby. For one terrible moment the man stood swaying on the edge of the roof, but then two firemen who had been waiting patiently for the right opportunity, dashed forward from the attic door, grabbed the man and helped him to safety.

The crowd below gasped its relief and when Margaret finally appeared in the doorway of the house she was given a tremendous cheer. The newspapers were full of her story the next morning and it was not long before she was invited to Buckingham Palace. There, in reward for her coolness, patience, understanding and courage, she received the George Medal from the Queen.

Perhaps her greatest reward of all, however, came when the man whom she had rescued recovered and thanked her for saving both his life and that of his son.
H5, P8, P16, P20

S5 Walking for others

Michael Sparks was a pupil at a school for mentally handicapped children in London. When a demolition order on the school building was issued, a group of parents formed a trust to raise money to buy and equip another house. This organisation was called the Noah's Ark Trust and one of the first people to help it was Michael's father, John.

He decided that one of the best ways by which he could try to raise money would be by doing a sponsored walk. He wrote to many firms and individuals who he thought might help. Then he set about doing the walk. From his first effort he raised £3,000.

During the next two and a half years John Sparks continued his good work. During this time he walked over 600 miles for charity and wrote 20,000 letters to firms and people asking them to support him. He walks during his holidays and has covered the Pennine Way (250 miles), the Cleveland Way (250 miles) and Offa's Dyke Path (168 miles). The Noah's Ark Trust certainly appreciate John's energy and help, for during this time he has raised £33,000 for them.
H1, P2, P25, P32

S6 Selfishness

Those people who care for pets and look after them properly find it hard to believe that there are others who just abandon their pets when they get tired of them. To do such a thing in England is punishable by law. The same problem exists in other countries too.

In Paris most people go on their holidays in August. It is at this time of the year that large numbers of pets are found abandoned and wandering in the streets. As many as 4,000 have simply been thrown out by their owners during the weeks of the holiday. One of the worst cases took place some years ago when a dog was taken to a wood in Paris and tied to a tree. Its mouth was then tightly bound with a bandage so that it could not bark. It would certainly have starved to death if someone had not found it and taken it to the police.

Once these animals have been rescued from their cruel circumstances they are taken to an Animal Home at Greenevilliers, a Paris suburb. Here they are looked after until someone adopts them and gives them a new home.
H5, P24, P29

S7 A place of worship

Enrico shivered in the bitterly cold northern wind and pulled his coat tighter round him.

'We could build the church right here if we tried,' he said.

His companions nodded in agreement. They were all Italian prisoners of war who were working in the bleak, northern part of the British Isles called Scapa Flow. Far from their homes and families, they wanted to build a church where they could worship together.

The only place they were allowed to use was a poor building with a curved roof, called a Nissen hut. The Italians, however, set to work to make it as beautiful as they could.

They collected scrap-metal from the many wrecks in the surrounding water and made altar rails, lamps, a crucifix and candlesticks. They carved statues from concrete and also built a belfry onto the front of the church with the same material. For months they collected old bits of broken glass and with them they made beautiful stained-glass windows. Some of the prisoners were good painters and they painted pictures and murals on the walls and the floor.

Eventually, what had been a desolate Nissen hut was transformed into an impressive, cared-for church. No sooner had the Italians finished, however, than the war ended and they were allowed to go home. But the local people of the Orkney Islands had seen this amazing transformation take place and, although the chapel is no longer used regularly, the islanders make sure that it is cared for. It remains a place to be visited and marvelled at. It is at Lamb Holm, Orkney.

H1, P1, P6, P36

S8 Salvage

To do something well means that the greatest possible care must be taken. In 1959 a British aeroplane called a Victor 11 crashed into the sea off the coast of North Wales. At the time it was the only Victor of this type in existence. It was new and people desperately needed to know what had caused the crash so that the defect could be put right on other Victors that were being built. Salvage ships were sent out to sea to recover the wreckage.

Once they reached the area where the plane had crashed, divers went over the side and the job of hauling up parts of the wreckage began. It proved to be a long and exhausting task, which was also very difficult. Finally all the pieces were collected and taken to a research establishment ashore, where they were painstakingly put together until the fault was located. It was estimated that, to do this, 500,000 pieces of the crashed plane had been brought to the surface by the salvage team.

H2, P11, P30, P43

S9 Echo

There is an old Greek legend about a girl called Echo. She was one of those people who always have to have the last word. If she was asked to do something she would always answer back, if she was discussing a subject with other people she always had to have the final say. In an argument she would never be first to stop.

Finally she was very rude to a goddess called Hera, who decided that Echo must be punished. The punishment was a severe one. Echo could no longer speak and say what she wanted, in fact all she could now do was repeat the last word anybody said to her.

Echo was so sad that she died fairly soon afterwards, but her voice remained behind for ever – and can be heard crying back in mountains.
H3, P3, P10, P28

S10 The poplar

Sometimes trees are like people; we can see so much on the surface but what we cannot see is often at least as important. The poplar is a tall, straight tree that is easy to recognise. Its wood is used for furniture, packing cases, matches, plywood and pulp for making paper.

Often, however, long lines of poplars can be seen planted along the sides of ditches and waterways. The reason for this is that the poplar's roots go down solidly into the earth and strengthen the banks of the ditches so that they do not crumble and fall in.
H1, P33, P44

S11 Well dressing

Despite the progress of recent years, some very old customs remain throughout the country. One of these is well dressing, where at certain times of the year local people go to wells and decorate them in thanks for past happenings.

The 'well dressing' is composed of panels of clay, dampened by salt water. This becomes a base onto which arrangements of leaves, flowers, bark, seeds, moss etc. are pressed. These things are skilfully put on to make up pictures of Bible scenes.

Some well-dressing ceremonies are reminders to give thanks for the water we use and need. At Tissington, in Derbyshire, one of the most famous well-dressing ceremonies is said to date from the fourteenth century, when people gave thanks for the village being spared when the terrible Black Death plague caused half of the population of the county to die.
P2, P9, P44

S12 If at first you don't succeed . . .

Ever since she was a very young child, the girl had been determined to be a pianist. Day after day she practised – scales with separate hands, simple tunes leading to more difficult ones. Eventually she became a marvellous player.

At sixteen she was already building up something of a reputation. She had over two dozen pupils coming to her for lessons and she regularly gave recitals throughout the district. She still spent as many as eight or nine hours a day practising. Then it happened.

One day as her hands were flying over the keyboard in a series of scales she felt a sharp pain in one of her wrists. It would not go away and she had to visit a doctor.

'I'm sorry,' the doctor said, 'the only cure is to stop playing the piano.'

'But it's my career, I've never wanted to be anything but a pianist!'

'All you will be able to do is play occasionally for your own pleasure, I'm afraid.'

Recovering from her terrible disappointment, the girl decided she would now become an actress. Starting right at the bottom again with small parts in amateur productions, she worked as hard as ever. Then she was able to become a professional actress. Her hard work again bore rewards. Soon she became known as one of Britain's most famous actresses. Her name was Dame Sybil Thorndike.

H1, P3, P6, P47

S13 An idea

Henry Meiggs was a young engineer from New York. In the middle of the nineteenth century he visited Peru and he had the idea of building a railway from the capital, Lima, up into the Andes mountains where there were rich copper mines.

People laughed at him – 'How could anyone build a railway to climb mountains that were higher than the highest in Europe?' Henry, however, was determined. His plan was to divert the water from a river and lay his railway tracks along the river bed so that the railway would twist and turn up into the mountains. Finally the Peruvian government agreed and work started.

8,000 men began moving earth and rocks, facing constant dangers from landslides. Then, after ten years' work, in 1879 war broke out between Chile and Peru. Work on the railway stopped at once. The half that had been completed fell into disrepair and it was eleven years before work could begin again. By this time Henry Meiggs had died, but there was now a fierce determination to complete the railway.

For twenty more years the work went on until finally the railway reached its highest point of 15,806 ft. Although it is less than 200 miles in length, the railway goes from Lima to its summit in the Andes via forty-one bridges and viaducts, round thirteen long hairpin switchbacks and through sixty-one rock tunnels. Large numbers of workmen are constantly employed protecting the track from landslides, avalanches, floods and falling rocks.

Henry Meiggs' idea became one of the world's greatest railway achievements.
P5, P11

S14 The soldiers' stamps

Stamp collectors are always on the look-out for rare specimens, but it is interesting to note that stamps have sometimes been the means of helping people.

Although Switzerland did not take part in the first world war, it was necessary for their army to be on guard against any possible invasion of their country. Soldiers in the army were allowed to send their letters post free. Then a man called Captain Bieri, who was an officer in the 38th Infantry Battalion, had an idea. As he was an artist he thought how much more interesting it would be if a special label or stamp could be designed to stick on the soldiers' envelopes to show that they were on 'active service'.

This idea was taken up and these labels were sold so that money from them could be given to a fund to help soldiers in need. Specimens of these 'soldiers' stamps' are now very rare.
P29, P33, P48

S15 The Ohio's last voyage

During wars many dreadful things happen – but some men show great courage and determination. During the second world war the island of Malta was being savagely bombed by German aeroplanes. To help the island's 270,000 people to survive, ships had to be sent from England with essential supplies, such as food and fuel. The Germans knew these ships were coming and did their utmost to sink them.

In August 1942, Malta had already suffered over 2,000 air raids and there was only a month's supplies left on the island. A convoy of ships set off from England. If they didn't get through, the island would have to surrender.

On 10 August the fleet of 14 merchant ships, 2 battleships, 4 aircraft carriers, 12 cruisers and 40 destroyers reached the Straits of Gibraltar. It was then that the Germans attacked. 21 submarines, 23 torpedo boats and 540 aeroplanes began continuous attacks on the ships.

After two days of the battle the oil tanker *Ohio* was almost a wreck. The wreckage of a German bomber lay on her deck, the steering gear was badly damaged, her gun barrels were worn out from constant use, holes covered the deck and sides. The captain had to order: 'Abandon ship.'

Knowing that the fuel the oil tanker carried was essential to Malta's survival the destroyer *Penn* took the *Ohio's* crew on board and then began towing the great tanker. Still the Germans attacked, but the *Ohio* refused to sink. With only 70 miles to go to Malta Captain Mason said to his men. 'Let's get back on board and take her in.' So the *Ohio's* crew clambered back onto their wrecked ship.

The Germans renewed their attacks, and 45 miles from home the *Ohio's* engine room began to flood. To aid the slowly sinking vessel another destroyer, the *Bramham*, joined the *Penn*. Supported by a destroyer on each side the *Ohio* struggled over the last few miles to the desperate island.

Meanwhile some of the other ships had reached Malta, and news of the oil tanker's struggle was passed round. Thousands of people crowded round the battlements of Grand Harbour. There, smoking in the distance, the incredibly damaged tanker could be seen, covering the last miles home with its faithful destroyer escort. A band began to play and wave after wave of cheers greeted the *Ohio* as she limped into the safety of the great harbour.

H2, P32, P35

S16 The collector

If you look carefully at the houses as you walk round London you can sometimes see small blue plaques which show that somebody famous once lived in that house.

Outside Number 4 Bloomsbury Place is a plaque with 'Sir Hans Sloane 1660–1753' written on it. Nearby is a part of London called Sloane Square.

Hans Sloane was a doctor, but it is as a collector that he is best remembered. When he visited Jamaica in 1687 he collected 800 specimens of animals and plants. All his life he collected and preserved specimens and records most carefully, and when he died he had 23,000 coins and medals, 30,000 books and 3,000 manuscripts.

In his will he left this amazing collection to the country and it became one of the main foundations of the British Museum. This museum is one of the most famous in the world and thousands of people have studied there. It owes its great reputation to men like Hans Sloane.

H1, P6, P22, P36

S17 Argument in the House of Commons

During the nineteenth century one of the Prime Ministers of England was called Disraeli. One afternoon Mr Disraeli was speaking to members of parliament and he told them that a certain 'Bill' was not to be discussed anymore.

At once a man called Samuel Plimsoll leapt to his feet and shouted out in violent protest. There was a great uproar and eventually Mr Plimsoll was warned by the Speaker of the House of Commons about his behaviour. Afterwards, however, many people wondered why Samuel had been so upset. He was only too keen to tell them.

Whilst living in Bristol, he had noticed that greedy and ruthless ship owners had overloaded their ships – but they made sure that the ship and the cargo were insured for more than they were worth. Often these overloaded ships went down at sea, with great loss of life. Samuel Plimsoll decided that this horrible practice could only be stopped if a line was painted round the sides of a ship. When the ship was loaded so that the water came up to this line, nothing more should be added or else the ship would be unsafe.

As an MP Samuel had worked hard on a Bill so that Parliament could make this a law – and Mr Disraeli had thrown it out! When Samuel explained this all again, more and more people began to see that he was quite right. Soon the Bill was re-examined and eventually a law was passed to say that all ships must have this line painted around them.

Ships still carry this line on their sides today and its name reminds us of the man whose determination to see justice done caused it to be put there. It was called the 'Plimsoll Line'.
H4, P5, P46

S18 Providing a home

When Charles II was King of England he was shocked to see so many old soldiers begging on the streets of London. All were desperately poor and many could not work anyway because of wounds they had received. Charles decided it was his duty to provide a home for such men. He ordered that a special hospital be built for them.

Sir Christopher Wren designed the hospital and it was built on what had been the Chelsea College, facing the River Thames. It is still there today and the old soldiers who live in it are called 'Chelsea Pensioners'.

Unless he is very sick, each of the 558 old soldiers who live in the hospital has a room for himself, and all eat their meals in the Great Hall. The hospital is supported by money given by Parliament and there is a governor, who is always a retired officer of high rank.
H3, P8, P15, P16

S19 The Incredible Journey

Most of us value our homes very much indeed. There is no doubt that the same applies to animals. In her book *The Incredible Journey*, Sheila Burnford tells the story of three animals who became homesick.

The owner of the animals, Professor Hunter, lived in Canada and was going, with his family, on a journey to England. So that his pets, Luath – a golden Labrador – Bodger – an old, nearly blind bull terrier – and Tao – a Siamese cat, – would be well looked after, Professor Hunter drove them 300 miles to the house of a friend.

When he had gone the animals were soon homesick. Despite the fact that they were being well looked after, they left their temporary new home at Longbridge and began the 300-mile journey back home across some of Canada's wildest country.

The animals must obviously have helped each other, and Luath as the leader must really have had to look after the other old dog and the delicate cat. Finally, after their incredible journey, the three animals arrived home very shortly after the Hunter family had themselves returned from England.

H2, P2, P8

S20 Justice

A pillory was a wooden post that had a wooden frame on top. In this frame were holes through which a man's head and hands could be put and locked into place.

Pillories were used to punish minor criminals. In 1266 a law called the Statute of Pillory said crimes such as perjury, forgery and shopkeepers cheating their customers would result in the guilty person being fastened in a pillory in a public place. This was usually a market square, and as people passed by they could throw unpleasant things at the person who was imprisoned in the pillory.

Gradually, however, pillories began to be used as punishment for different kinds of offences. There is a famous story connected with this. Daniel Defoe was a great writer, and in 1703 he wrote a pamphlet saying that the government should allow people much more freedom to worship God in the ways that they thought best.

As a result of this, he was sentenced to stand for one hour in a pillory at Cheapside in London. Then an amazing thing happened. Many people who had read or heard about his pamphlet thought he was right, and very courageous for saying what he had done. And so, they all came along to the pillory and hung and threw flowers all round Daniel. They told others why they were doing this and Daniel's courage was rewarded

when, instead of being jeered and pelted as a criminal, he was cheered as a hero.
H4, P13, P15, P45

S21 Overland rescue

The winter of 1881 was one of the worst ever known in the North of England. One night of sleet, snow and howling winds the news flashed round Whitby that a ship – the *Visitor* – had gone aground six miles further up the Yorkshire coast at Robin Hood's Bay. The *Visitor* was a small brig with a crew of only eight, but they were all Whitby men. The news was that they were adrift in the Bay in a small ship's boat. Unless a lifeboat could get to them they had no hope of survival.

Lifeboats at this time, however, were rowed, and in this kind of storm there was no chance of being able to row from Whitby harbour to Robin Hood's Bay. The only thing to do was to take the lifeboat on its carriage overland to the Bay and launch it there. The road over the moorland country was, however, covered with snow.

Undismayed, the people of the town got to work. A large group of men, armed with lanterns and shovels, went ahead to clear the roads as best they could. Meanwhile thick, long ropes were attached to the lifeboat carriage and a crowd of men, women, children and horses began to pull the enormous weight over the steeply sloping roads. At one point there were fifty horses and dozens of people all hauling desperately. In and out of snowdrifts, over icy patches, along parts where the road was almost too narrow, the strange procession moved.

News reached the struggling people that the *Visitor's* boat was still afloat but didn't look as if it could be for much longer. In desperation a decision was made to leave the road and pull the lifeboat across country in an effort to get to the Bay more quickly. The group with the lanterns and shovels now knocked holes in moorland walls so that the boat could get through. Finally the beach at Robin Hood's Bay was reached. It was covered in ice and so dangerous that the helpers now had to strain to hold the boat back so that it did not slide out of control into the sea.

Manhandling it to the water's edge, the crew got aboard and, riding out on the next huge wave, they rowed furiously towards the exhausted men in the *Visitor's* boat. The courage and determination of all were rewarded when the lives of the entire crew of shipwrecked seamen were saved.
H5, P20, P34, P37

S22 Modern life

One of the reasons why we should be grateful that we live today instead of in years gone by is that over the centuries men have learned many things that help to make our lives safer.

Now we have laws to protect us and no-one is punished for wrongdoing without a fair trial. This was not always the case. The ancient Britons had terrifying ways of deciding whether or not a man was guilty of a crime. Instead of a fair trial the accused was tested by either fire or water.

If he chose water, he was tightly bound and thrown into a river. If he sank he was considered innocent. If he floated he was thought to be guilty and was taken out and executed.

If he chose fire, he had to carry red hot bars in his bare hands for three paces. If this caused his hands to blister – and it obviously almost always did – he was considered guilty.

We should be grateful to people like King Alfred who, hundreds of years ago, realised that such measures were cruel and foolish, and appointed judges to listen to witnesses and evidence so that they could decide whether or not a person was guilty of the crime of which he was accused.

H3, P9, P14, P17

S23 When paths cross

The captain of the British gun boat saw the slave-ship trying to mount more sail to make its escape. A shot across the bows put a stop to that, and soon the terrified cargo of negro slaves was being taken back to West Africa and set free.

One of them, Samuel Crowther, went to a church school there and showed very quickly that he was an extremely clever scholar. After being baptised he eventually became a priest and then a missionary. He founded many churches in Nigeria and when it was decided that the country needed a bishop, Samuel Crowther was the man chosen.

To become a bishop is a great honour, and Samuel had to travel to Canterbury cathedral for his consecration. At this service, a very old man in the uniform of an admiral sat and looked on with pride. He was the sea captain who, forty years before, had saved the thirteen-year-old Samuel from being taken away to a life of slavery.

H1, P1, P23, P46

S24 John Newton

All sorts of different people are, and have been, Christians. John Newton, who was born in 1725 was captured by a Press gang when he was a young man and forced to be a seaman.

He was constantly in trouble at sea. He regularly refused to obey orders, deserted at least once, and was very unpopular with his captains. In 1748 a ship he was on was sailing from America to England when it ran into a terrible storm.

The ship was soon in desperate trouble. The pumps were manned and John and his fellow sailors struggled to plug leaks in the ship's sides. At one stage the captain was so sure that his craft's troubles were because he had such a bad character as John in his crew that he had almost decided to throw him overboard. Finally the storm eased and the ship limped homewards.

Being saved from the storm had a great effect upon John. When he went back to sea he became an ideal, hardworking and reliable sailor. Gaining steady promotion, he soon became a captain himself. Then he left the sea and after studying hard became ordained as the Vicar of Olney in Buckinghamshire. Not content with this, he took a great interest in missionary work and spoke to many people about what Christianity really meant. One young man who listened very carefully, and became a friend of John's was William Wilberforce. In a short while he became very famous indeed for his work in ending slavery.

P4, P14, P28

S25 To share or not to share

Two travellers were walking along a road. Suddenly one of them noticed a nearly-new axe lying in the gutter. He picked it up.

'Look,' he said, 'now I've got an axe.'

'You mean "we",' said the other traveller. 'I thought we shared everything.'

'Nonsense,' replied the first man.

Before many minutes had passed there was the sound of horses' hooves behind the travellers. Three horses galloped up to them. The rider of the first horse shouted out.

'There it is. He's the one who has got my axe.'

'Oh dear,' said the first traveller, 'now we're in trouble.'

'Not "we",' replied his companion, 'you.'

H4, P15, P45

24 Stories

S26 Shame

Philip, father of Alexander the Great was one day warned that one of his leading officers was plotting against him. After listening to the charges, Philip thought for a while and then came to a decision.

That night he held a great banquet and the officer was invited as guest of honour. During the course of the banquet Philip looked him straight in the eye and presented him with a medal for his past services. Afterwards the officer was so ashamed of what he had been plotting that he gave it up and became again one of Philip's most loyal followers.
H3, P28, P41, P48

S27 Greed

A poor fisherman sat by a river bank one day, whistling as he fished. He whistled so beautifully that a fairy princess heard him. Instantly she appeared beside the fisherman.

'Marry me and I'll make you rich and handsome,' she said.

'Right,' said the fisherman, and with a wave of her wand the fairy transformed him into a handsome young man dressed in magnificent clothes.

'Before I come with you, may I go and say farewell to my friends?' asked the fisherman.

'Of course,' replied the fairy princess, and as she clapped her hands a coach and horses appeared on the spot.

Driving into the city, the coach had to pass the palace where the queen of the country lived. Seeing the handsome man in the great coach, the queen had it stopped and asked the rich-looking passenger to drive with her.

Afterwards the two of them went to the palace and had a magnificent meal. During this the fisherman thought to himself, 'The queen is young and lonely. She thinks I am handsome and rich. If I marry her I'll be king of the whole country. That's even better than going with the fairy princess.'

So, forgetting the promise he had so recently made, the fisherman, being as charming as he could, asked the queen if she would marry him.

No sooner had the words left his mouth than he was transformed back into an old fisherman, clad in dirty and smelly clothes. The queen had him thrown out at once.
H5, P22, P31

S28 The Colosseum's last victim

Forty thousand people crowded into the Colosseum in Rome to celebrate the great victory over the Goths. Although early Christians were already growing in number and trying to persuade people to help stop the senseless killing in the great arena, the crowd were excited at the thought of savage battles.

Animals were hunted and killed, but when the gladiators emerged from the narrow passages leading into the arena, another figure was suddenly to be seen. There, amidst the swords and spears of the gladiators was an old man. He was dressed in simple clothes and was barefoot. Shouting to the front ranks of the crowd, he pleaded with the people to leave and to save the lives of those who would be killed before the afternoon was out.

Furious at the thought that somebody might spoil their entertainment the great crowd jeered and threw stones at the old man. He was a hermit called Telemachus. Finally one of the gladiators came across and struck him a savage blow with his sword. Still pleading with the crowd, Telemachus dropped to his knees, and then finally fell to the ground and lay still.

When the crowd realised that the old man was dead, a sudden hush stilled the shouting. Ashamed at what they had been urging, people began edging towards the exits. Soon the great arena was empty – and never again were the savage slaughters held there.

H4, P5, P12, P23

S29 Helping out

The Church of England Children's Society finds homes for children who otherwise would not have one. One of these homes is in Merseyside, and the children who live in it are aged from six months to fourteen years.

When the people and firms of the area heard about these children, they set about helping in the best way they could. A local engineering firm gave a junk car for the children to play in; a group of workers from the local telephone exchange arranged to take the children on regular visits to the seaside; a group of men at the nearby Vauxhall Motors factory raised money to provide transport to take the children on holiday; many local people sent invitations to Sunday School parties, barbecues and other local events.

The housemother who looks after the children said how grateful she was to all these thoughtful people.

H3, P16, P18, P26

S30 The boy who succeeded

When Peter Howard was born, his left ankle was joined to his knee. Doctors operated on his leg and although they managed to straighten it out it was twisted and thin and they thought Peter would be a cripple all his life. For many years he wore an iron support on his leg. Then, because he was determined to play rugby, he took off his leg iron and began to play the game.

Despite his lame leg Peter became a brilliant player and eventually became captain of the England rugby team. During this time he had another shock when a motor cycle he was riding collided with a lorry. Seeing that his motor bike was too badly damaged to ride Peter borrowed a bicycle to ride to hospital as his lame leg was giving him some pain. When he got there, after a twelve mile ride, doctors found that the leg was broken in two places.

Peter eventually became a very important Christian leader who travelled all over the world speaking to groups of people. By his own great courage he set them a fine example.

H4, P7, P12, P47

S31 A true story from a local school

Jenny had moved house. She had no brothers or sisters and had come to live in a completely strange place. On her first day at school she found most of the other children had their own friends and were not very bothered about her. Only one girl, Maureen, really took the trouble to speak to her properly all day.

That night Jenny fell on the stairs at home and had to have her leg put in plaster. Obviously she could not go to school, and as neither she nor her parents knew anyone in the district she was very lonely. Meanwhile Maureen had found out what had happened.

She hardly knew Jenny and she could have forgotten about her until she was better; she could have sent a 'get well' card and left it at that; she could just have sent her something to read.

Instead, Maureen got all her friends together and told them what had happened. Then she arranged for a collection of things for Jenny to read. Next she and her friends went to see Jenny. They gave her some magazines and comics and arranged to come back and see her in ones and twos until she was well enough to get back to school.

H5, P1, P2, P39

S32 Hospitality

Because of its bleak climate, terrible storms and lethal offshore icebergs there is a saying that Labrador was the country that was made 'last of all'.

Wilfred Grenfell was an English doctor who spent his life there, working for the Royal National Mission to Deep Sea Fishermen. Regardless of the terrible climate, he claimed that the people there were amongst the kindest in the world.

He told a story of how one night he was exhausted after a long and difficult day. He called at a house and immediately both the man and his wife got out of bed to welcome him in. They gave him hot cocoa to warm him up and then insisted that he went straight to bed.

It was only later that Grenfell discovered that the couple were extremely poor. The cocoa had come from a specially treasured hoard and they had only one bed in the house. Whilst he had slept in it the man and his wife had lain on the floor.
H2, P32, P38, P48

S33 The greatest sacrifice

Nathaniel Saint's first great disappointment in life was when a US Air Force doctor told him that because of a weakness in the legs he could not train to be an Air Force pilot.

Recovering from his disappointment, Nat began training at a College for Christian missionaries. He enjoyed his course and then discovered that, to reach people in isolated places, an organisation called Missionary Aviation Fellowship was being formed. After further training Nat became a pilot/missionary. His first posting was to Equador.

From the airstrip on its edge Nat flew supplies to missionaries who were deep in the jungle. Occasionally he flew out desperately sick people who needed hospital treatment.

After seven years Nat could speak several Indian dialects. He particularly wanted to contact a tribe known as the Aucas. He wanted to try and persuade them to give up their practice of killing any strangers who approached them.

With other pilots, he flew over Auca territory, dropping gifts and food to the Indians below. Finally he landed at an Auca village and, because he could speak some of the language, he was able to exchange greetings.

Delighted with his success Nat then flew back to his headquarters and arranged for four other missionaries to fly with him deep into Auca territory. After a radio call to say that they had landed safely there was a long silence. Next day a search was organised. The bodies of Nat and the others were found near a river. All had been stabbed by Auca spears.

Deciding that it would have been what the men wanted, Nat's sister, Rachel, and one of the other missionary's wives, Mrs Elliot, then went into the jungle to find the Aucas. After making contact, they managed to live with this fierce tribe. Eventually their example of love and forgiveness won the Aucas to a more peaceful way of life.

P3, P12, P14

S34 Saved

The passengers of the DC8 Alitalia flight were full of praise for the crew of the plane when they landed in Beirut in June, 1970. This had been no ordinary flight.

Over Syria the plane had suddenly found itself in the middle of a dogfight between Syrian and Israeli jets. Hit by a stray rocket, the DC8, which was carrying 104 people, suddenly went into a dive after a loud explosion. The left wing was a mass of flames and pieces of debris flew past the passengers' windows.

With great skill the pilot, Captain Giorgio Pizzo, regained control and switched off the outer port engine. Meanwhile the cabin crew calmed the terrified passengers. Eventually the plane landed at Beirut. It had a huge hole in its left wing, the flaps were not working, and fuel was pouring out of damaged feed lines.

The passengers all agreed that they owed their lives to the courage and skill of the DC8's crew.

H5, P30, P33, P44

S35 Kindness

An old lady who lived by herself had just enough money for essentials. There was nothing to spare for any luxuries. One day she was in a greengrocer's buying her vegetables when she noticed a basket containing some beautiful carnations. The only other person in the shop with her was a rather untidy-looking young man.

Without being able to take her eyes off the lovely flowers Mrs Danton bought her sparse vegetables. She kept thinking about how delightful just one of the carnations would look in her rather dark, drab flat.

'How much are they?' she asked the assistant, pointing to the flowers. When she received the answer she knew she could not afford even one.

She left the shop and began the long walk home. Before she had gone far she heard running footsteps behind her. Turning round she saw the untidy young man hurrying to catch her up. In his hand he held a small bunch of the carnations.

When he reached her he said just two words: 'For you.' Then leaving Mrs Danton holding the flowers he was gone as quickly as he had arrived.

H1, P1, P2, P7

S36 Quick thinking

Terry Corr is a train driver and his very responsible job is made much more worrying than it should be by the barrage of missiles thrown by vandals. Even worse, these people sometimes put obstructions on the track. This could cause a serious derailment.

On one occasion Terry was driving his train on the main Newcastle-upon-Tyne and Teesside line when suddenly he saw an old car seat lying across the track ahead. Because he could not stop in time Terry's engine was derailed and the whole train halted in a highly dangerous position.

Realising that the next train along would crash into his and many people would probably be killed or injured, Terry acted quickly. Taking a red flag from his cabin he raced 200 metres back along the track and waved down the next train. The driver slammed on the brakes and managed to stop just a few metres away from Terry's derailed train.

H2, P28, P36

S37 Douglas Bader

The biplane's engine roared as Douglas brought it nearer to the ground. He began a spectacular roll, which caused the pilots who were watching to gasp in admiration. Then it happened!

One of the wing tips touched the ground and an instant later the plane was cartwheeling and disintegrating over the runway.

When Douglas awoke in hospital he knew he had been seriously hurt. A sympathetic doctor came to tell him that to save his life both his legs had been amputated. When the doctor had gone Douglas gritted his teeth and thought to himself: 'I am going to learn to walk and then I'm going to fly again.'

Some years passed and after tremendous efforts Douglas taught himself to walk, and even play golf. He refused to use any sticks and used only his artificial legs. Then the second world war began, and Douglas applied to join the RAF as a pilot again. Many times he was told that he could not but he showed himself to be so determined that eventually he succeeded and he became a Spitfire pilot.

Soon he became an 'ace' and won the respect of his enemies as well as his friends. On a mission over France his Spitfire was hit by enemy fire and he had to bale out. No sooner was he taken prisoner than he tried to escape. When he was re-captured he said to the Germans that it was his duty to try and escape and he would continue to try and do so at all times.

Despite the fact that he had only artificial legs, the Germans were so afraid Douglas would succeed in his escape attempts they decided to put him in their special escape-proof camp – Colditz Castle.

Eventually the war ended and Douglas returned home. His fame was international and everyone admired his courage and determination. He has made great efforts to encourage other handicapped people to live lives as fully as they possibly can.
P30, P35, P46

S38 Retired?

When Joe Armstrong retired he had definite ideas about what he wanted to do. Various people spoke to him about having a 'well-earned rest' now that he was sixty-five. He smiled and nodded but rarely said anything.

After visiting several large villages he finally found what he wanted. This was a small house with a large garden. He and his wife moved in. Shortly afterwards neighbours were astonished to see a railway coach being towed through the streets. Eventually it was taken into Joe's garden and fixed securely into place.

For the next few weeks Joe was very busy fixing book shelves in the carriage. The next surprising event was the arrival of a van bringing hundreds of books. These Joe arranged on the shelves of his railway carriage.

Finally Joe announced that his book centre was open for all children to use. He had chosen his books well and they were the sort children enjoyed reading. The thrill of reading and choosing them in a railway carriage added to the attraction and the reputation of Joe's 'Book Centre' spread rapidly. Soon children and their parents came from a wide area to see, read and enjoy.

When Joe was complimented on what he had done for the children he brushed such statements aside. 'They've done far more for me,' he would reply.
H3, P31, P38, P47

S39 The mean and foolish king

There was once a king who was mean and cunning. This king's greatest pleasure was listening to stories. He soon tired of the storytellers in his palace and was always looking out for someone who could tell new and interesting stories.

Eventually there came to the country over which the king ruled a man who could tell wonderful stories. Soon news of his reputation reached the king. The storyteller was sent for.

When the king heard the man's first story he enjoyed it enormously. Being mean and cunning, however, he pretended that he had not been over impressed.

'Well, it wasn't bad,' he said. 'I want you to come back every night of the week and see if you can improve.'

The man did so. Each night he held the king fascinated with one marvellous story after another. Not once did the king allow his enjoyment to show. He fidgeted and yawned and scratched, and paid the storyteller a fraction of what he was worth.

Finally the storyteller told the king that he would have to leave the country and find a job somewhere else.

Angrily the king told him he did not know when he was well off, and if that was how he felt he should go.

The storyteller left, was never heard of again by the king, but made a fortune in another land. Meanwhile the king, despite his great riches, could never again find anyone to give him the pleasure the marvellous storyteller had done.

H1, P42, P45, P47

S40 Justice?

In the year 339 BC the famous Greek philosopher Socrates was on trial for his life. His 'crime' was advising the young people of the state to think for themselves and not necessarily follow in the path of their elders.

A tribunal of senior citizens passed judgement by voting, but, before they did so, lawyers sought to prove that Socrates was guilty of 'corrupting the young'.

Socrates spoke in his own defence and made a telling point. Even the prosecution admitted that he was not a fool, and, so said Socrates, as it was pleasanter to live amongst good people how could he be foolish enough to try to 'corrupt' them and have to live amongst bad people?

In conclusion Socrates warned the tribunal that in the long-term his death would do more harm to them than would his acquital. Nevertheless, he was found quilty by a vote of 281 to 219 and sentenced to die by drinking poison.

His death helped to strengthen people's belief in the wisdom of his teaching.

H3, P35, P41, P43

32 *Stories*

S41 Charity

In many prosperous countries there now exist charitable organisations which seek to help quickly when disaster strikes in countries that cannot help themselves.

In 1970, for instance, a cyclone caused a five-metre high tidal wave to sweep inland in Bangladesh. There was no sea wall to bar its progress, and in the floods that followed 250,000 people died. The government could provide little help.

When a disaster like this strikes, the Disasters Emergency Committee (made up of five British charities – Christian Aid, British Red Cross, Oxfam, Save the Children and War on Want) meets. They use the BBC and ITV to launch immediate appeals; charity representatives liase with the government of the country concerned; they assess the needs of the survivors; they locate and purchase the necessary supplies; emergency requirements are investigated and an effort is made to see that those who are in the greatest need are given help first.

H5, P39, P40, P44

S42 Another chance

The famous sculptor was hard at work. He was feeling particularly happy because he was just finishing one of the finest small figures he had ever made. With a sigh of satisfaction he put the last touch of paint on it and said to one of his assistants, 'Alfredo, please, very carefully take this upstairs and put it in the box of straw so that it can be delivered to our rich customer.'

Alfredo, taking great care, took the beautiful figure from his master. The sculptor turned back to his bench, but as he did so he was horrified to hear a crash. Alfredo had dropped, and broken, the statue.

Many men would have been furious, and shown it. The sculptor paused, then turned back and began collecting the materials to make another identical figure.

A week later he had finished. He called to his assistant, 'Alfredo, please take this carefully and put it in the box upstairs.'

P27, P33, P48

S43 Sincere

Old time craftsmen who worked in marble used a clever trick on their unsuspecting customers. If the marble had a flaw in it they melted wax and put it in the flaw. They then polished the piece very hard so that it was impossible to detect the wax. Next they tricked the customer by selling the piece to him and claiming it was perfect.

Eventually this trick came to be well known and buyers insisted on guarantees, signed by the craftsman to say his work was free of wax. CERA was the old Latin name for wax. SINE was the word for without. Thus the guarantee said: SINE CERA (without wax). From these words we get our word: Sincere.

H2, P21, P28, P45

S44 Humility

When Doctor William Nkomo died, in March, 1972, he had become so famous that more than ten thousand people attended his funeral. As a black South African he was known throughout the world for his hatred of violence and his desire to see men of all kinds treated equally.

During his life he had worked tremendously hard for South Africa so that it might be 'a hate-free, fear-free, greed-free continent, peopled by free men and women'.

Despite the fact that he was very famous and greatly respected, however, Dr Nkomo had not forgotten what it was like to be poor, and he cared for the poorest person he knew in the same way as he cared for everybody else.

He proved this by his actions as a doctor. In his whole lifetime of helping sick people he never gave any of them a bill for his services. They paid him what and when they could.

H4, P24, P29, P35

S45 Preparation

Ravenscar is a village on the North Yorkshire coast. It stands high on top of the cliffs and even in summer a cold wind often blows in off the North Sea. There is a footpath that leaves Ravenscar for a place called Osmotherly. This footpath is forty-two miles long, it travels right over the moors, and it is called the Lyke Wake Walk.

Even in summer this is not the sort of walk that should be made without careful preparation. Fog and mist often cover the moors quickly and an inexperienced walker can soon get lost and become exhausted. Unfortunately, there are still many people who do not prepare themselves properly for such a walk. These people often go missing so that the Moors Rescue Team has to be called out to go and look for them.

When a walker is reported missing, the National park Warden rings up the members of the Rescue Team. These are all people who know the moors well. They meet at an arranged spot and carry First Aid kits and food, as well as being properly dressed for the walk. They have compasses to find their way, and carry whistles. Once they are out on the moors they blow their whistles to let the lost walker know that they are searching for him.

Often they find that a walker has sprained an ankle by putting a foot in a hole when it is hard to see. The Rescue Team then has to use a Land Rover radio to send for an ambulance.

By giving up their warm beds to spend cold, wet nights searching the lonely moor, the Moors Rescue Team have saved many lives.
H2, P14, P37

S46 Carelessness

The twins got a puppy for Christmas. They were delighted. 'Let's call him Sooty,' said Jill as she looked at the brown eyes in the black face.

The puppy flapped his ears and seemed to nod in agreement.

'No, I think we should call him Tiger.' said Jonathan.

Well, they still had not agreed on the puppy's name when they took him out for his first walk. He jumped around on the end of the leash and bounced up and down like a fluffy black ball.

When the twins arrived at the park, lots of children were there. They all crowded round for a look at the puppy. Then they showed Jill and Jonathan their presents. After a while Billy Jones said Jonathan could have a go with his kite, and Angela Simpkins said Jill could have a ride on her new bike. So Jill tied the puppy's leash round the metal base of a swing.

Now there were some children using the swing and as it whizzed backwards and forwards above his head the puppy got quite excited, and leapt up and down. As he did so he weakened the knot, which Jill had not tied very well.

In a flash he was loose and jumping up to catch the swing, but then he realised it was coming towards him much quicker than he had thought. There was a loud crack as the swing hit the little puppy on the head; he fell to the ground and lay still.

'Jonathan!' Jill screamed as she saw what had happened.

All the children ran to the tiny, still little dog on the ground. There was no sound from him.

A lady, who lived near the park, had seen what happened and she took Jill, Jonathan and the puppy to the vet's in her car. At first the vet was not too happy at being disturbed on Christmas Day, but when he saw the puppy he got straight to work.

After about ten minutes he returned to the waiting room where Jill, Jonathan and the lady sat. He looked very stern.

'Well, he's going to be all right – but I hope that you have learned your lesson and never do anything as careless as that again!'

'Oh, we won't,' said Jill, trying to hold back the tears of relief. Jonathan could only nod.

So the puppy made a complete recovery and the children looked after him very carefully for ever after. You might like to know that as they talked about this that night Jill said to Jonathan, 'I hope he'll forgive us.'

'Me too,' said Jonathan. 'Let's give him a name made up from "Forgive us."'

So they did, and even when the little black puppy grew up into a handsome dog he was still called 'Fus'.
H5, P17, P28, P43

S47 The Albert Medal

The Albert Medal was instituted by Queen Victoria in 1866 to reward civilians for acts of bravery in peacetime.

One of the most astonishing stories associated with its award took place in 1916. Eight-year-old Doreen Ashburnham and Anthony Farrer, aged eleven, set off from their home on Vancouver Island to collect their ponies. When they reached the paddock they saw the terrified ponies crowded in a bunch whilst a puma snarled at them.

Before the children could do anything the puma saw them and attacked. Doreen was immediately pinned down by the beast. Without hesitation Anthony began to lash the animal with his riding whip.

Infuriated by this the puma leapt off Doreen and attacked Anthony. Doreen then got to her feet and went to the boy's aid. Pulling and scratching its back with her bare hands she managed to distract the beast from savaging Anthony. Finally, confused by the continued resistance of the two children, the puma retreated, snarling, to the woods.

Bleeding from numerous bites, scratches and wounds, the children mounted their ponies and rode home. Several months later the Governor-General of Canada awarded them both the Albert Medal – the only children to receive it.
H4, P12, P20, P29

S48 Thought for safety

When fierce storms threaten the lives of crew on damaged ships we usually hear stories of great courage shown by those who man Britain's lifeboats. Perhaps we should appreciate more how some of their equipment came into being.

In February 1807, a small ship was caught in savage seas off the coast of Norfolk. Among the helpless watchers who saw both ship and crew pounded to destruction was a man called George William Manby.

As he left the terrible scene Manby thought of how many lives could have been saved if some sort of life-line could have been got to the ship's crew.

The same year he borrowed an army mortar gun and practised shooting lines over various distances. His invention greatly impressed the Suffolk Humane Society and within a year the device had already saved the lives of the crew of a sinking ship called 'Elizabeth'.

By 1810, mortars and lines were established on various parts of the coast, and by 1823 Manby's idea of firing a life-line to sinking ships had saved over 200 lives.

H2, P34

S49 The right present

A lady called Jean visited her uncle who was now living in an old people's home. She found him feeling rather sorry for himself and not much interested in whatever she had to say.

As she went home afterwards she remembered how clever Uncle Jim used to be at making things. She had an idea for her next visit.

A week later Jean arrived again to see her uncle. This time she talked about the paper flowers and model aeroplanes and miniature toys he had made and carved when he was younger. The old man nodded at the memory but said he 'could never get stuff like that now'.

Jean smiled to herself, but didn't say anything. When she left she made sure that the parcel she had brought was on a table in the entrance. The parcel had her uncle's name on it. Inside the wrapping was a number of coloured sheets of paper, some balsa wood, a craftsman's knife and other modelling materials.

A week later she came back – and what a difference she noticed. In the room where she talked to her uncle there stood on the table a vase containing some paper flowers which were so beautiful that she thought they were real. Beside them was a half-finished carving of a small dog.

'Jean, I can't thank you enough,' said Uncle Jim. 'Not only have you got me interested in my favourite hobby again, but two of my friends here want me to show them how to do these things too.'

H3, P15, P16, P18

S50 Actions or words?

Have you ever thought how difficult it would be to communicate with somebody when there was not one single common word of language.

Nevertheless this sort of barrier can be overcome.

In 1979, when so many Vietnamese people had to leave their own country because of the terrible things that were happening there, a large number of overcrowded boats put to sea.

A British ship picked up one of these boat-loads of Vietnamese people and brought them to England. The refugees were very grateful for their rescue but they could not talk to the ship's crew because they did not have any common language. On arrival in England, there were no houses for them to go to, and the only place that could be found to give them shelter was an old unused army camp. It was drab and cold and after the warmth of their own country the Vietnamese found it frighteningly strange.

The army camp was near a village and although the villagers wanted to make these strangers welcome nobody knew how to do it. Then one of the villagers had an idea.

It was the village church's flower festival and the beautiful old church was full of flowers of every kind, size and colour. On the Monday after the last Sunday service of the flower festival a fleet of cars drove up to the church. Villagers got out of their cars and very carefully took down the flowers and then drove with them to the old army camp.

When they got there they spent the next few hours decorating the army camp as painstakingly as they had decorated the church. They may not have had the words to show that they cared about their new Vietnamese neighbours, but their actions certainly did it for them.
H2, P40, P41, P44

S51 A Bible story (from Luke 12)

Once upon a time a rich man's farmland produced an enormous amount of crops. This made him think: 'What shall I do with it all?'

Then he thought, 'I know, I'll pull down the barn I've got and build two or three much bigger ones. Then I'll cram all the grain into these and I'll never have to worry again. I'll have plenty of good things stored up for years and years to come. I can just relax, forget about work and do nothing but enjoy myself. What a good time I'm going to have.'

That night when the man went to bed he died.
H4, P7, P13, P17

S52 Thought for others

Two letters that appeared recently in a woman's magazine showed how much people appreciate thoughtfulness. In one of the letters an elderly woman described how she spent a great deal of her time knitting cardigans for her friends and relatives. One of her friends was particularly fussy about a cardigan when asked if she wanted one. The sleeves had to be a special style, the buttons had to be just right, the wool had to be of the finest texture.

Finally it was finished, and the friend took the cardigan away. Next day the old lady who did the knitting received a parcel. Opening it she found inside the cardigan she had just knitted. Attached to it was a note which said: 'Thank you for all you have done for us – we wanted this one to be for you.'

The other letter concerned a grandmother who did not have much money and could not get out very easily. She asked her granddaughter for some envelopes for Christmas, as she loved writing letters. She was delighted when she received some writing paper, and a large supply of envelopes – with every one stamped ready for use.
H3, P1, P15, P16

S53 Be what you are

Once upon a time there was a donkey called Dick. Drinking in a stream one day, he noticed a gleam of yellow. Looking more closely, Dick saw that it was gold. He was rich!

Now Dick had never cared for being a donkey. He would have much preferred to be a horse. Now that he was rich he could do something about it.

First of all he had his ears trimmed. Next he had his coat smartened up. Now he not only began to look like a horse, he felt like one too.

He began to go around with other horses. He did not even bother to speak to his old friends amongst the other donkeys. Finally came Dick's greatest moment. He was invited to a horse party.

Well it was a really good party. They galloped and jumped and chased each other around. At last it was time for everybody to go home.

'Before we go,' neighed the horse whose party it was, 'let's finish with a song.'

Dick joined in with the rest. Suddenly he noticed that something was wrong. All the horses had stopped neighing their song and were looking at him.

Then he realised what was the matter. He might look like a horse, he might feel like a horse, but when he opened his mouth he could only be a donkey.
H2, P31

S54 Freedom

Sometimes in Britain we take freedom for granted. For other people, however, freedom can often only be won by doing something very dangerous. On 17 September 1979, the newspapers told the story of one daring deed in search of freedom.

Hans-Peter Strelzyk lived in Poessneck, East Germany. With a friend, and their wives, Hans secretly built a balloon. It was made by stitching sheets and curtains together and the hot air to fill it came from four gas cylinders.

Finally they decided to attempt their escape. Waiting until it was dark, they filled the balloon with hot air. Then, with their children, aged fifteen, eleven, five and two, they climbed into the basket.

Slowly the balloon rose into the darkness and at 3,000 feet it soared towards West Germany – and freedom. Below, minefields and self-firing guns threatened death if the balloon came down too soon. After thirty minutes it began to drop.

Hardly daring to get out the escapees looked round anxiously to see where they were. Then they saw a police car – but it contained West German policemen. They were safe!

H3, P5, P19, P44

S55 An ordinary home

There is a small town in Norfolk called Walsingham. In 1061 the Lady of the Manor there had a strange dream. In her dream she received instructions to build a house like the one in which Jesus spent his boyhood in Nazareth. When this was built people came from miles around to see it. They continued to do so until 1538 when the king ordered this shrine (as it was called) to be destroyed.

After its destruction it lay in ruins from 1538 until 1921. Then a new shrine was built. Inside a large and beautifully decorated church a small house, just big enough for a family to live in, was built. To the many thousands of people who visit it, this is a reminder that Jesus lived in a small, and very ordinary, house just like most other people do.

P8, P36, P37

S56 The legend of the stag

It was a cruel winter. The harsh wind cut across the land and the flakes of snow were driven hard before it. The stag looked at his herd and knew that to survive they must go in search of fresh food. Waving his proud head with its large antlers, he led the herd through the driving snow.

On and on they went, occasionally finding food and always encouraged by their leader. None of the animals knew that the giant stag was eating nothing. He was making sure that all his herd got enough to eat, and, this done, he found that there was nothing left for him.

Finally they reached a more sheltered hillside. Seeing that this was a good place for his herd, the giant stag lay down to rest. Overcome with tiredness and lack of food he died during the night. But that is not the end of the story. On the spot where the leader died, his antlers gave birth to a tree with a fine bark, which fed herds of deer on this hillside ever afterwards.

H2, P32, P33

S57 'Fidelity'

If you go to England's Lake District and approach the country's third highest mountain (Helvelyn) from Patterdale you must walk along Striding Edge, a narrow pathway between two precipices. It is an easy walk in summer but a dangerous one in winter.

Not far from Striding Edge is a monument which recalls a sad but moving story. The monument was erected in 1890 by Canon Rawnsley and Miss Coombe in memory of Charles Gough's dog. Charles Gough was walking up on the mountains one day in 1805. He had not told anybody where he was going and his only companion was his dog. Near Striding Edge he fell and was killed.

For three months his body lay undiscovered until finally, a shepherd came across it. The astonishing thing was that the dog, now desperately thin and weak, was still there on guard beside its master's body.

William Wordsworth, a poet who loved Lakeland, wrote a poem about this story. He called it 'Fidelity'.

> The dog had watched about the spot,
> Or by his master's side;
> How nourished there through such long time
> He knows, who gave that love sublime;
> And gave the strength of feeling, great
> Above all human estimate.

H2, P4, P24, P48

S58 Gratitude

Waltham Abbey is a beautiful old church that stands in the centre of a busy little Essex town. As the traffic bustles by it is hard to imagine the strange legends associated with this building.

Hundreds of years ago a mysterious jewelled cross was found on the land of a man named Lord Tovey. He ordered it to be taken to Waltham for safe storage and the heavy cross was dragged there in an ox cart.

The famous 'holy cross' of Waltham became a local legend and in the middle of the 11th century King Harold decided to come and see it. He was suffering from paralysis and, in hope of a cure, he arrived at Waltham and prayed before the cross. Miraculously the king *was* cured.

He was determined to show how grateful he was for this cure so he ordered the building of a great church. Today the old church still stands there, and people have worshipped in it for over nine hundred years.
H5, P9, P14

S59 Oberammagau

Four hundred years ago the villagers of Oberammagau decided that they would give thanks because their village had been spared in the epidemic that had killed the inhabitants of so many other villages in Southern Germany.

They decided to produce a Passion play every ten years. This custom has continued ever since, except in war time. All the villagers play a part; the stage is open but the audience sits under cover. The performance lasts six or seven hours and takes place in two parts – morning and afternoon. A fanfare of trumpets that echoes round the mountains means that the performance is due to start.

Visitors who come to see the play stay with the villagers for two nights. They are allowed to stay in a villager's home on the night of their arrival, they see the play the next day and stay in the same home that night. They must then move out to make way for other people.
P44, P47

S60 Faith

In a very cold province forty Christians were captured by the persecuting Romans. The Roman governor took them down to a frozen lake, made them take their clothes off and forced them to walk onto the ice until it cracked and they were up to their necks in freezing water.

Any who would renounce Christianity could come out. None did, so the governor had a bonfire built on the shore as an added incentive. One Christian gave up, came out, and was allowed to go free.

The next morning troops came to take the thirty-nine frozen bodies from the lake. To their amazement they found forty bodies. One of the Roman soldiers had said to himself: 'If that is what being a Christian means then I want to be one.' So saying, and unseen by his comrades, he had joined the martyrs in the lake, bringing their number back to forty.
P10, P13, P40

S61 Contentment

John was a watch repairer. He was not very good at his job and could only just make enough to keep his family. He worked at home. Living in the same house were his wife and three children.

One day John was talking to a friend who was considered very wise. John was complaining about the noise and commotion his wife and children made. He asked how he could possibly be expected to work well with them around him all the time.

The wise friend advised John to get a bird, and then come back and see him in a week's time. John wondered how this would help, but he got a bird. Its chirping and singing nearly drove him to distraction when he was trying to concentrate. He told the wise friend this when he saw him a week later.

'Right,' said the wise man, 'get a cat as well and come back and see me in a week's time.'

A week of torture followed for John. His bird was noisy, the cat was constantly trying to get into the cage to eat it, the children were especially excited. Next week the friend listened to John's complaints.

'Get a dog,' he said, 'and see me in a week's time.'

The next week was a nightmare. The bird was noisy, the cat tried to eat it, when it was not dodging round the furniture to escape the dog which was chasing the cat. The children joined in the chasing and the noise. A week later John was almost distraught.

'I can't stand a minute more of it,' he said to the wise man.

'All right, sell the two animals and the bird,' answered his friend.

John did this. It was marvellous to get back to something like peace. What had he been complaining about in the first place?
H5, P31

S62 Old Age skills

Age Concern is an organisation that seeks to help old people. One of its most interesting ideas was to support a man called Edward Walton who had a brilliant idea called 'Link Opportunity'.

This works as follows: imagine that you are a retired lady who is an excellent cook, but can no longer do any heavy gardening. Joe, who lives alone in the same town is also retired, is a fit and keen gardener, but cannot cook. Where Link Opportunity is in existence both you and Joe could ring them up and explain what you could do, and what you wanted done.

Joe might them be asked to tend two or three small gardens. For doing this he would be paid in credit stamps.

You might be asked to bake cakes – and be paid in credit stamps.

With some of the stamps Joe might buy your cakes; with some of your stamps you might buy some of Joe's time to do your garden.

The scheme helps old people socially and also gives them the chance to practise their individual skills and retain a pride in them.

H4, P2, P13, P18

S63 The gift

One day two of the gods came down to earth and began moving invisibly amongst the people. As they passed by a poor man's house they heard the sounds of crying from inside.

'What is the trouble in there?' asked one of the gods.

'Ah,' replied the other, who knew, 'it is the house of a poor servant. He has no money, a mean master, and no food to give his wife and children.'

'Hmm,' replied the first god. 'Tonight we will leave him a store of gold inside his front door.'

As luck would have it this conversation was overheard. The person who heard it was the master for whom the servant worked. At once he made his way to the servant's house.

'Now my man, I want to buy this house,' he said. 'I'll offer you 5,000 crowns.'

'But sir . . . began the servant.

'All right . . . if you are going to argue, I'll give you 10,000.'

The servant, who could hardly believe his ears, began to speak again, but his master cut him short.

'There is one condition though – you and all your family must be out of the house within an hour.'

So the servant, still not able to believe his good fortune, left his ramshackle old house with enough money to buy a better one and feed his family for weeks.

The master moved in. Later that night the gods went by.

'Do you remember,' said the second god, 'we were going to leave a fortune for the poor servant tonight?'

The first god nodded wisely. 'I think he's already got it,' he said.

H1, P18, P23, P39

S64 Think before you act

A man had two sons. He gave them each a quantity of pea pods and asked them to get the peas out. The first son split the pods, filled the bottom of a large bowl with them, and then put the peas on top. There looked to be a large bowl of peas.

The second son split the pods, put the peas in one bowl and the pods in another. Then he took the bowl containing the peas to his father.

Without giving the second son any chance to explain the father raged at him for producing only half the peas that his brother had brought in his bowl.

The second son was so upset that he left home immediately. The father was left with the other son – and he quickly found out about his deceit. By now however it was too late to correct his mistake.

H3, P7, P15, P17

S65 Pulling together

A farmer wanted to be able to collect his two horses quickly. So he tied them together with a piece of rope.

One of the horses decided he would go and eat at the western side of the field. The other horse decided he wanted to go and eat at the eastern side. They set off in opposite directions and soon the rope grew taut between them. Pulling and straining neither could make the other budge. Soon they were not only hungry but sweating and exhausted.

Suddenly one of the horses said to the other, 'Why don't we walk together and eat at the western side, then go over and eat at the eastern side?'

Common sense had at last prevailed.

H3, P17, P27, P45

S66 Learning all the time

Every year new and exciting things happen. For instance, in 1909 Bleriot made the first cross-Channel flight, landing at Dover on 25 July; the

Victoria and Albert Museum opened; roller skating arrived; in the English towns the new craze was whist drives; a new act refused children under fourteen entry into public houses; in the USA the first mechanical roadsweeper was introduced; the moving staircase was introduced in the Paris Metro and guillotining took place again at public executions.

How important it is to benefit from the good things of every year, and equally to learn from its mistakes.

H1, P5

S67 Be a man of your word

A tiger was trapped in a cage. A goat came along.

'Goat, please let me out of this cage. I've been trapped here for days,' the tiger called out to the goat.

'I won't do that,' said the goat. 'If I do, I know that you will eat me straight away.'

'No, no,' said the tiger. 'I will be very grateful, and I promise I will do you no harm at all.'

The goat released the tiger, who immediately siezed his benefactor and prepared to eat him. A jackal was passing by. The goat called out for help and quickly explained what had happened.

'I don't believe any of it,' said the jackal.

'What do you mean by that?' asked the tiger.

'Well for a start I don't believe that you were ever trapped in that cage.'

'Oh,' replied the tiger, getting angry.

'Of course not,' continued the jackal, 'you couldn't even get in that cage, you're too big.'

'Well I was in it,' snarled the tiger, 'and I'll prove it.'

So saying, he climbed back in the cage. At which point the jackal and goat slid the bolts back into place and went on their way.

H5, P15, P20

S68 The slave painter

Juan de Pareja was a negro slave who lived in Spain in the 17th century. When he was young his mistress died and he was 'inherited' by her nephew, the famous painter Don Diego Velazquez.

Slaves could, of course, be treated exactly how their masters wished, but Velazquez was kind to Juan. As the great painter's fame grew, the couple became familiar figures at court, where Velazquez did many paintings for King Philip IV.

Juan's job was to prepare the materials and studio for his master. Eventually, however, he became fascinated by the artist's work and, selling an earring of his mother's which was his only possession, he bought some materials of his own and began to paint in secret.

Some years later the King was visiting Velazquez's studio. Suddenly he saw a canvas lying, face to the wall. Turning it round he saw that, although it was very good, it was not the work of the great artist. Juan's secret was out.

Legally still a slave, Juan feared some dreadful punishment for his secret activity. Seeing Juan's distress, Velazquez asked the king's permission to write a letter there and then. Then he gave the letter to Juan. The contents proclaimed that Juan now had 'all the rights and honours of a free man', and it appointed him as the artist's official assistant.

Juan never forgot his master's generosity – and now he was free to paint in his own right.

H3, P26, P29

S69 St Giles

Many churches in Britain are dedicated to St Giles. An interesting characteristic about these churches is that they are usually situated in what was once the outskirts of cities. This is because St Giles, who was said to be lame himself, is the patron saint of cripples. The churches bearing his name were originally built in places through which poor and lame travellers would pass on a journey from the countryside into a town. The church named after this saint in the City of London is in Cripplegate.

Giles was supposedly an Athenian, born in the eighth century. Leaving his home he settled as a hermit near the mouth of the River Rhone in France. Legend claims that a deer, fleeing from the King of the Visigoths, ran to Giles' hermitage for protection. The king was so impressed with the serenity of Giles' existence that he gave him some land and arranged for a magnificent monastery to be built on it. Giles became the abbot of this monastery.

P18, P31, P48

S70 Man overboard!

Arne Nicolaysen was a seaman on the merchant ship *Hoegh Silverspray* in 1955. Working on deck in the winter of that year, the young Norwegian was caught off balance by an unexpected roll and plunged overboard.

Despite his shouts for help nobody heard him and soon he had the terrifying experience of seeing his ship sail out of sight, leaving him alone in an empty sea. He was off the coast of Florida and the water was not too cold, but Arne knew that this was shark territory.

Pulling his socks half off, he hoped that the movement of them as he floated would scare off the sharks, which can sometimes hesitate about attacking. Hours went by as he struggled to stay afloat. Meanwhile, not until 9 pm was Arne missed aboard the *Hoegh Silverspray*. The captain immediately sent a signal: 'man overboard, all ships alerted', but he felt sure in his own mind that Arne was hopelessly lost.

By now Arne was fighting to stay alive in the darkness. Almost exhausted, he would fall asleep, only to be awakened by a choking mouthful of water. With the arrival of dawn Arne could see ships passing, but his ever weakening shouts for help went unheard. By now his eyes were almost closed and he longed for a drink.

Then, as another day drew to a close, a seaman on board the passing British trawler *Surveyor* saw a limp figure in the water. A boat was lowered and soon Arne was safe on board. The captain could hardly believe the young seaman's story. He had managed to stay afloat in the sea, without a life jacket, for twenty-nine hours. It was an amazing feat of courage and endurance.

H4, P34

S71 Man of honour

King Louis IX of France lived in the violent times of the Middle Ages. Despite the fact that he was neither particularly strong nor particularly clever, he became one of the most repected kings in Europe.

This was because, above all things, he was a man of real fairness and honesty. It was his custom in the summer to go into the woods at Vincennes on a Sunday. There he would sit on the same fallen tree trunk every week so that any ordinary citizens could go to him with their troubles. If a subject had suffered an injustice, Louis did his best to put it right, even if it meant he or one of his nobles was in the wrong.

He sent judges all over the country so that people could have the opportunity of getting justice. He daily provided large quantities of food for beggars, and arranged for a hospital to be built in Paris to cater exclusively for the poor.

Despite the violence that often surrounded him, Louis, by means of this consideration for others, greatly helped the sufferings of the poor. Twenty-seven years after his death in 1270 he was made a saint.

P7, P13, P15

S72 Determination

Polio is a disease that leaves people with thin, twisted and weakened limbs. When she was two years old Doris Hart had polio so badly in one of her legs that doctors at one time considered amputating it.

They decided not to, but as she grew up Doris suffered pain from the leg and was only able to move with a sort of awkward, dragging movement. Her greatest ambition, however, was to be a tennis player. As she grew older she practised hard, was coached by an expert and taught herself that quick thinking could sometimes compensate for the fact that she could not move as quickly as other players.

Gradually Doris became an excellent player. Now she had another problem. Appearing before thousands of people who saw the difficulty with which she moved was not easy. Doris conquered this worry with her usual determination, and finally came the greatest day of her life.

In the 1950 Wimbledon championships she met Shirley Fry in the women's final. She played so well that she won, 6–1, 6–0. Not content with this, she partnered Shirley Fry to win the women's doubles; and with Frank Sedgeman she won the mixed doubles. The girl with polio had won the greatest of all tennis honours – the Wimbledon Triple.
H1, P1, P6, P10

S73 The Dickin Medal

The Dickin Medal is the Animals' V.C. (short for Victoria Cross – a medal awarded for bravery). In 1945, when the Second World War ended, a Victory Day programme was broadcast by the BBC. One item on this programme was the barking of a dog – but this was no ordinary dog.

Judy was a nine year-old pointer who had once been the mascot of a Royal Navy ship. During the war this ship, HMS *Gnat*, was sunk by Japanese bombers. The crew managed to get ashore to an uninhabited island nearby. There, after a time, they began to die of thirst. Judy, however, who had swum ashore with them, finally dug out a fresh water spring that was usually covered by waves. At last the sailors had water.

Soon, however, the whole group was captured by the Japanese and put into a prisoner of war camp. Conditions in the camp were dreadful, but Judy saved several lives by barking warnings of approaching poisonous snakes. Once she even fought off a crocodile that was creeping into the camp.

When the war ended, Leading Aircraftsman Frank Williams brought Judy back to England on a troopship. After six months in quarantine she was awarded her medal. With every medal there is a citation which says why it was awarded. Judy's said that her medal was for: 'saving many

lives through her intelligence and watchfulness'.
H5, P32, P40

S74 Courage

To be a leper in years gone by was to live in terrible circumstances. Apart from the pain and disfigurement of the illness, lepers were shunned and driven away by their fellow men. There was even the humiliation, in some areas, of having to call out 'Unclean' as they walked.

But some people had the courage to face up to this dreadful disease and try to do something about it. Daniel Danielssen was a Norwegian doctor who was born in 1815. In an attempt to find out if the disease was really infectious, he injected into his own body the matter from a leper's sore, and then some leper's blood. Neither of these experiments gave him leprosy. Next he transplanted a leper's infected skin under his own. Still he did not catch the disease.

As a result of Danielssen's work the first steps were taken to prove that leprosy was not always infectious – but only in certain areas and in certain conditions. Today, although leprosy has still not been eliminated, there are drugs called sulphones, which clear up its symptoms. In many countries, although lepers still have to be isolated, they are given treatment, good food and facilities.
H4, P12, P16, P35

S75 A lesson learned

A merchant once had to make a long journey. Before he started this, he sold all his property and possessions for gold bars. He thought this would be the safest way of retaining his wealth.

He then asked a close friend to lock the gold bars in his treasure chamber.

A year later, when the merchant returned, he went to his friend's house. The friend greeted him with an air of apology.

'I've got bad news, I'm afraid. Would you believe that rats got into my treasure house and ate every single one of your bars of gold?'

The merchant looked sadly at his so-called friend. He knew the man was lying of course, but he had trusted him and therefore had no proof that he had left the gold in his charge. Quietly the merchant shook his head, said, 'How unfortunate,' and made his way out of the house.

Just outside the house he saw one of the deceiver's children playing. There was nobody about so he picked up the boy and took him to his own home.

Hours later there was a terrific knocking on the merchant's door. There stood his friend.

'My son! He's missing, we can't find him anywhere. We've been searching for hours. Have you seen him?'

'Well, you know, its an amazing thing, but as I left your house I saw a sparrow swoop down and carry your son off.'

The distressed father looked at the merchant for a minute and then lowered his head in shame. Within the hour both the gold bars and the child were returned.
P10, P23, P45

S76 Saved

Many years ago, a Frenchman retired and went to live in his villa overlooking a wide river. There, he would sit on the terrace and gaze out across the river. One morning he saw a horseman approach the other side. Suddenly the horse reared up and the rider was flung into the river.

Seeing that the man was in danger of drowning, the Frenchman, forgetting his age, plunged into the river to help. After a terrific struggle with the heavily-clothed and hooded horseman the Frenchman finally got him to safety on the river bank. Then, pulling back the other's hood, he gasped in astonishment. He had saved the life of his own son.
H3, P2, P4, P33

S77 The good sleeper

In the days when men out of work were hired at annual fairs, a farmer went to hire a labourer. Questioning the row of men waiting to be hired he got a variety of answers.

'I am a good man with sheep,' said one.

'Take me for ploughing,' said a second.

'I'm the best for sheep shearing,' said a third.

The farmer was most intrigued with the man who said, 'I sleep well at nights,' He hired this man.

Later that year a terrible winter storm savaged the farm. Next morning the farmer told his labourer how he had spent a sleepless night worrying. 'I kept thinking of the wind tearing the tops of those hayricks.'

'I slept well,' said the labourer. 'I knew they'd be all right. After all, I put them on.'
H5, P22, P36, P39

S78 The rewards of generosity

Cyrus, King of Persia, was known to be an extremely generous king. One day, another far richer king, who was staying with him said, 'If you continue to give away your wealth like this you will eventually become very poor. Imagine how much wealthier you would have been if you had kept all the riches you have given away.'

'If I had kept all that I have given away, how much do you think I would now have?'

The visiting king thought about Cyrus's question, and then be began to carefully work out the answer. Soon he named an enormous sum.

'Right,' said Cyrus. 'I will send servants round to all my friends and subjects. I will tell them that I need money urgently.'

This was done. A few days later Cyrus sent for his guest. Taking him out into a courtyard he showed him an enormous pile of gold, and gifts. It was worth far more than the sum the visiting king had named.

'There you are,' said Cyrus. 'If I had hoarded all my money my people would have hated and resented me. As it is, by helping them as much as I could, I can get far more by simply asking for it than I could have saved. Far more important it shows that I have the respect of my subjects.'

H1, P13, P21, P25

S79 Fair play

Three beggars lived in a dark and dingy cave outside a town. They decided it would be easier to live if they shared what food they had.

After deciding upon this, they went their separate ways to beg for the day. The first beggar was given a potato, the second a piece of cooked meat with a large bone in it, the third a pile of carrots.

Coming back to the cave at night they lit a fire and put on their cooking pot, filled with water. Now, each said, a potato, meat and carrots should make a fine thick soup.

With a splash the first begger put in his offering, followed by the others. An hour later each sipped a spoonful and tasted – only hot water.

Shamefully the three of them took out the stone, the cleaned bone and the carrot tops they had put in the pot. Going to three separate hiding places they recovered the potato, meat and carrots and put them in the cooking pot. They had learned their lesson.

H1, P17, P19, P28

S80 The small things

It is easy to persuade ourselves that small things do not matter. How wrong we can be in this sort of thinking is shown in this story.

A Boeing 707 was approaching Calcutta on a flight from London. Everything on the plane appeared to be working properly and, although it was foggy, there seemed no reason why it should not land safely. Inexplicably, it crashed just before landing, killing the pilot, co-pilot and twenty-seven passengers.

A month's investigation finally revealed the cause of the crash; a small screw in the altimeter was loose – it had not been screwed in properly.
H5, P11

S81 Give a dog a bad name

An elderly lady wrote a letter to a magazine, expressing her opinion about football crowds. She lived very close to a ground and had come to dread Saturday afternoons. She was frightened of the noise, the traffic and particularly the surging, jostling supporters.

One day she was out shopping and forgot that there was a match on. To her horror she found herself, complete with heavy shopping bags, caught up in the frenzied rush to reach the ground in time for the kick off. It was a very cold icy day and, in her hurry, she suddenly slipped. Not only did she have a nasty fall, but the contents of her two shopping bags went flying all over the pavement.

At once a group of young football supporters, covered in badges and scarves and cheering noisily, stopped to help. They collected all her belongings up and then escorted her right to her own front door.
H3, P2, P5, P45

S82 Consideration

The Depression was a period in the 1930s when millions of people were out of work and short of money. One lady told a story of how a group of unemployed men gathered together in a long street to sing. They sang beautifully, and then one of their number made a house-to-house collection to get money for their families.

When he called at the lady's house she reached for her tin of coins and gave him one. When he had gone she realised that she had given him the wrong coin – for an amount she couldn't really afford.

Later that night there was a knock at the door. It was the man who had done the collecting. He had found the lady's coin on the top of the

pile, realised it was far more than she could afford, and brought it back for her.
H1, P2, P18, P20

S83 Do you feel sorry for yourself?

Famous author Aldous Huxley went blind in later life and had to use braille to read. Various people were concerned at finding the great man in this situation. He dispelled this concern by his cheerful demeanour.

'Think of the advantages.' he said. 'You can read in bed under the blankets, and even on the coldest nights your hands stay warm!'
H4, P12, P17, P31

Class Assemblies

Like the rest of the book, this section aims at providing practical suggestions. The assemblies described could be re-enacted as written or they could be starting points for new interpretations. They seek to offer a wide variety of presentation and take heed also of the progression, events, highlights etc. of the school year. Whilst many could be adapted for use at any time, suggestions of which months might be best suited for each presentation are included in the 'Reminders' section of this book.

56 *Class Assemblies*

A1 **Take it from here**

In many ways a good assembly can be likened to a memorable piece of music where 'the melody lingers on'. There is a definite place for the sort of assembly that presents a series of visual and aural effects, with none of the traditional inclusions of hymns and prayers, but with a vast opportunity for related follow-up work in the various classrooms. Assemblies such as this encourage observation of certain features which can then be developed by teachers with their classes afterwards.

An example of this type of assembly could be built round a subject that most children find of great interest, such as 'Flags'. The aim of the presentation, which could be made by one class, would be to supply as much information as possible, but also to leave ample scope for follow-up work.

The presenting class could initially be divided up into several groups. Each group would be given a brief for research. The assembly would then consist of about six themes set within the major theme of 'Flags'. Each group would have a visual display linked to spoken passages, mimes, tape recordings, short plays or whatever is thought most appropriate. Thus the contents of each group's work might be as follows:

Group 1

The aim here would be to show that information is useful in living. For instance, there is an international code of flag signals for every letter. (See illustration.)

The point could be made that spelling a message out letter by letter is a very slow process and it is speeded up using the combinations of letters that have special meanings (for details of these see *The International Code of Signals*, pub. HMSO).

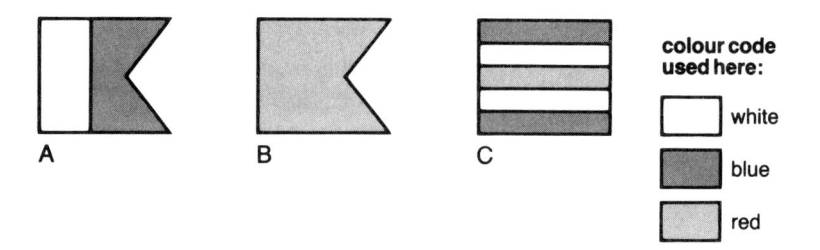

Group 2

This group's brief could be to show how useful flags are to give warnings. They could paint and show the flag of vertical red and yellow stripes that warns motor racing drivers of oil on the track, and the red flag flown by ships warning that they are carrying explosives.

Group 3

This group could use their display of flags, and commentary, to show how flags are used to express courtesy, in honour of foreign visitors; or when a ship entering a foreign harbour flies the flag of the host country as a mark of respect.

Group 4

Group 4 could show a large representation of the Red Cross flag. (See illustration.)

The group could tell how it signifies internationally that help is being given. More details of Henri Dunant and the founding of the Red Cross could be given here.

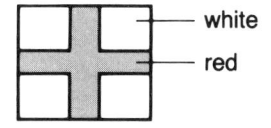

Group 5

It is an easy progression of thought from the idea of needing help to that of wanting peace, and this group could concentrate on detailing some situations where the white flag is shown.

Group 6

This group could continue the theme to include flags that denote peace, unity and mankind linked for the good of each other. Two possible illustrations here could be the Olympic flag of five interlocking rings in which each ring represents a continent, and the flag of the United Nations Organisation, which consists of a blue background and a white world encircled by white olive branches.

These displays, and appropriate comment, could conclude the assembly but they could also sow the seeds for a great deal of work to be done later. For instance it is a small step from showing a flag symbolising 'Help' to considering local organisations that provide help for people in various ways. Obviously much valuable local research could be done on this.

Similarly, flags could be considered under a 'signs and symbols' theme, which might lead to a study of signs and symbols in Christianity – cross, altar, candles, various facets of churches, emblems of different saints etc. This could lead to carefully planned visits to local churches.

Finally, one of the great benefits of this kind of assembly is that it often inspires ideas in another classroom, which can ultimately lead to another assembly presentation by that class. Thus the circle of thoughts, ideas and progression is maintained.

Sources

Piccolo Picture Book of Flags by Valerie Pitt.
The Schoolboy's Pocket Book by Carlton Wallace, pub. Evans.
Both of the above are useful for details about flags and messages. For more ideas on unusual and thought-provoking assemblies a good source is:
Celebrating Together – a resource book for Primary Assemblies, by Peter Wetz and Pauline Walker, pub. Darton, Longman and Todd.

A2 Qualities

The only 'prop' for this assembly would be a mirror. When the children are assembled, two of the presenters could step forward to a prominent position. One could then hold up a mirror whilst the other looked into it. Having done so, the viewer could then turn to the audience and say:

'A man called E.A. Guest once said, "I want to be able, as days go by, Always to look myself straight in the eye."'

A second speaker could then step forward from the presenters with another comment:

'We think Mr Guest meant that we should never do anything we are ashamed of. Our assembly this morning looks at some stories to make us think about this.'

A group could then present, in shortened narrative and mime form, the story of the Pied Piper. Emphasis should obviously be placed on the dishonesty of the mayor in the action. A second group could then re-enact a Biblical scene. A good choice here would be the story of the king and the governor, in which the king, in a moment of compassion forgave a governor a debt of £1,000,000. The same governor, only a short while later, ruthlessly imprisoned a man who owed him £5. This is ideal material for a simple play, or as an alternative, it could be mimed to a reading of the story from Alan Dale's 'New World'. The Bible reference here is Matthew 18: 23 – 34.

By this stage in the assembly qualities of honesty and compassion will have been drawn to the children's attention in a memorable manner. Other desirable qualities, seen in contrasting situations, could then be illustrated by a short selection of readings and poems. Included in these could be the salutary poem 'Timothy Winters' by Charles Causley, and one or two of the passages included in this book. Particularly suitable here might be: 'Fidelity'; Faith; Think before you act; Be a man of your word; The slave painter. (*S57, S60, S64, S67, S68*).

Once this point of the assembly has been reached, the singing of a hymn could fulfil two useful purposes. It would involve the participation of all and it could alter the emphasis of the assembly. A hymn appropriate for both purposes is 'Gifts', which is included in the hymn section of this book.

Following the singing of the hymn, there could be a longer than usual section of the assembly given to thoughts and prayers. The first part of this might be used to re-iterate some of the qualities it is desirable for all of us to possess, and which have been illustrated in the mimes, poems and readings.

From this it could be said that Christians believe that desirable qualities are strengthened by their belief, and the examples that Jesus gave. Many people feel, therefore, that prayers are a means of gaining strength. The assembly presenters could then remind the audience that people have been praying for hundreds of years and that there are many old, traditional prayers.

An example of a beautiful old prayer could then be used. One choice might be the prayer of St Richard of Chichester:

> Day by day,
> Dear Lord, of thee three things I pray:
> To see thee more clearly,
> Love thee more dearly,
> Follow thee more nearly,
> Day by day.

The service might end with a prayer that reminds all that the theme has been about personal qualities:

Lord, forgive us for our selfishness and lack of concern for others,
For our thoughtlessness in not seeing what needs to be done,
For our forgetfulness, which causes people to be hurt and offended,
For deliberately avoiding opportunities to help in many ways.

Sources

New World – The heart of the New Testament in Plain English by Alan T. Dale, pub. OUP.
Assembly – Poems and Prose, compiled by Redvers Brandling, pub. Macmillan is one source for 'Timothy Winters'.

A3 Enough for all?

This assembly could be used at any time of the year, but perhaps it would be most appropriate at Harvest time or when some work is being done on Third World countries. It can be presented by very young children and the emphasis is very much on visual impact.

Before the service starts it is necessary to have a collection of various things. These include some pictures of the consequences of lack of food in underdeveloped countries; some pictures of successful farming in Western countries; some photographs of children in obvious good health; some ingredients for a common meal in Britain – eggs, bacon, bread, butter, jam etc.

It is also necessary to make some large letters on separate pieces of card. These should be big enough to be seen quite clearly at the back of the hall when held up, and the letters need to be: AEHRSTV.

The display boards containing the photographs should have their blank sides facing the audience initially. The presenters could take up their positions and the assembly might begin with everybody singing: 'When I needed a neighbour'.

At the conclusion of the hymn one of the presenters could say: 'Our neighbours in less fortunate countries than ours need our help in many ways. Look.'

At this point, one of the boards displaying Third World deprivation pictures could be turned round to face the audience. There could then be some comment that people in these countries can not get enough food and therefore many of them will starve. As this point is being made six of the presenters, having practised getting into place beforehand, could move into position carrying six of the large letters which spell out:

STARVE

There could then be some comment by another group of presenters. Their theme would be that not all the world is so unfortunate and we are well off for food. Whilst these comments are being made other children could turn round the display boards revealing pictures of harvesting in the western world. At this stage the plates showing the ingredients for a meal could be brought in too. Then someone could say: 'With what we have we can help people who may otherwise starve.'

In conjunction with this statement the children carrying the letters of STARVE re-arrange themselves and are joined by another child carrying the letter H. When he takes his place at the end of the re-arranged line, the caption should now read:

HARVEST

A speaker could now say: 'We can help others by sharing our crops; by giving expert advice on farming methods; by collecting money to buy useful machinery.'

An assembly such as this depends so much for its success on its visual message that further prayers or readings could be thought superfluous, particularly with very young children. It might be better, therefore, to conclude the service with a suitable record playing and allowing some extra time for all the children in the audience to file out slowly past the display, having a closer look at it as they do so.

Sources

For visual material concerning Third World countries: Christian Aid, PO Box No. 1, London SW1; Oxfam, 274 Banbury Road, Oxford; Save the Children Fund, 29 Queen Anne's Gate, London SW1.

'When I needed a Neighbour' is in *Come and Praise*, the BBC hymn book (from BBC, 35 Marylebone High Street, London W1M 4AA. A linked record of the same name is on BBC REC 317).

A4 The most dangerous animal in the world

We all like mysteries and an assembly that starts with a puzzle is sure to intrigue everyone. In this instance, a very large cardboard box should be in place, in front of the presenting group, as the rest of the children enter the hall. This box should be covered with 'stickers' such as: 'Highly Dangerous!' 'Beware!' 'Not to be opened!'

Once everyone is settled in the hall a question and answer routine can begin the assembly:

'This box contains a very dangerous animal.'
'What animal is that?'
'It is the most dangerous animal in the world.'
'Is it a tiger?'
'No.'
'A snake?'
'No.'
'What is it then?'
'The best way to find out is to open the box.'

At this stage two children leave the group and start to open the top of the box. This needs to be done slowly and carefully, and when completed, the boy who has been inside the box stands up to reveal his head and shoulders. He then speaks.

'What is all this nonsense? I'm just an ordinary person. I'm not the most dangerous animal in the world.'

A reply from one of the presenters is then forthcoming:

'You represent "Man", and he is the most dangerous animal in the world. If you look and listen you will see why.'

The presenting group then begin to elaborate with a series of statistics, comments and mimes. These are aimed at showing that one of the greatest threats to the world is pollution and it is man who is responsible for this.

I saw a 3rd/4th year junior class, guided by a perceptive teacher, present this theme. The mimes started with local interests and spread to more major issues. The progression went from the litter that constantly needs to be cleared from around the school; housewives struggling to keep clothes and houses clean in dirty environments; a car load of passengers depositing litter on the countryside; a ship at sea emptying waste.

At the conclusion of these mimes and comments, a series of prayers and thoughts could be read. Many of these could be written by the children themselves and they might compare the beauties and benefits of nature with what man is doing to them by his carelessness. The service could then be concluded by the singing of a relevant hymn. A choice from any of the following would be appropriate here: All things bright and beautiful; O Lord, all the World belongs to You; Think of a World without any Flowers; Come let us remember the Joys of the Town.

Sources

For the hymns suggested in this assembly, 'All things bright and beautiful' exists in numerous anthologies; 'O Lord all the World belongs to You' can be found in *Sing Life, Sing Love*, pub. Holmes McDougall; and both of the other hymns are in *New Orbit*, pub. Galliard.

On the problem of pollution, a useful address is: The Conservation Society, 246 London Road, Earley, Reading R96 1AJ.

A5 Bible story

B.W. Hearn, in the excellent book *Religious Education and the Primary Teacher*, says of assemblies that they 'must never be rushed or undignified. Must be serious but not lack humour; never be pompous, pretentious or flippant; should never lack vitality and sincerity.'

Obviously, few teachers would quibble with this statement, but achieving its aims regularly is not easy. Many would feel this to be particularly so when relying on traditional sources. It is possible, however, if the right interpretations of traditional sources are used, and a little imagination is applied to visual aids, to produce interesting and worthwhile assemblies from these beginnings.

One of the best introductions to such an assembly that I have seen came from a lower junior class. Once the rest of the school were in the hall this group made their entrance to some 'joyful' music (Pete Seeger's 'If I had a hammer' in this instance), and took up their places, leaving three of their number in an exposed position holding large cards with the blank sides facing the audience.

The service then began with one of the children turning her card round to reveal that it contained a large letter 'J'. The other two then showed their cards, on which were written letters 'O' and 'Y'. The mutterings of 'Joy' from the audience allowed the presenters to move straight into the reasons why they had begun their service like this.

SPEAKER 1   To feel joy is to be happy.
SPEAKER 2   Our happiness and contentment often depends on other people.
SPEAKER 3   We enjoy the company and kindness of friends.
SPEAKER 1   We get pleasure from giving as well as getting.
SPEAKER 2   Let us look again at letter 'J'.

Once again the letter 'J' was brought to the forefront and this time one of the presenters reminded everybody that J could stand for Jesus. The letter 'O' was then brought back into position beside the 'J' with the comment that O could stand for 'Others'. We were then reminded that the stories of Jesus showed that he thought a great deal about others and taught people that this was the way we should all think. 'Y' was next brought into place with the comment that by following 'J' (Jesus' words and teaching) and considering others ('O') joy could come to you yourself ('Y').

The stage was then set for some short mimes and readings of one or two appropriate stories told by Jesus. For brevity and language most suited to children of this age group, Alan Dale's *New World – The Heart of the New Testament in Plain English* is an obvious choice for Biblical material, and it was used here.

This particular service concentrated on the issues above but an assembly similar to it could certainly be extended to involve another traditional source rarely considered at all by primary school teachers. This source is the psalms.

Usually psalms are incomprehensible to primary school children but

Psalm Praise, by Michael Baughen, contains psalms in language much more appropriate to this age group, and well suited for use in periods of prayer in assembly. An example illustrating this could be taken from Psalm 121, which in this book reads:

> I lift my eyes
> To the quiet hills
> In the press of a busy day.

If 'traditional sources' have been used for an assembly of this nature, a contrast could be to learn and sing a modern hymn as a finale. One ideally suited to this theme would be 'Give me Joy'. An alternative to this could be a reading of the very thought-provoking poem, 'Joy', which is included in the 'Thoughts and Prayers' section of this book.

Sources

'If I had a hammer' is one of an excellent selection of useful folk songs to be found in 'More Folk in Worship', by the Crown Folk on BBC record REC 176.
Psalm Praise, by Michael Baughen, pub. Falcon Press (Falcon Court, 32 Fleet Street, London EC4Y 1DB).
One source for the hymn 'Give me Joy' is *New Orbit*, hymn anthology, pub. Galliard.

A6 'Happiness Hill'

The success of the 'Mr Men' series with infant children could provide a starting point for an assembly with children of this age-group which should make them think.

Pre-assembly classroom preparation on this occasion should be quite detailed and result in the production of several visual features essential to the service. The first of these would be a large frieze. The main feature of this frieze would be a hill. Centrally positioned and surrounded by 'countryside', this would be labelled 'Happiness Hill'.

The children could next make a series of card figures, of the right proportion for use with the frieze. These could be painted/drawn in a way to suit their names. The latter could be attached to each.

When the frieze is in position for the assembly the figures should have been arranged on either side of 'Happiness Hill' and stuck on by means of 'Blu-Tack' or a small piece of double-sided sellotape. One group of the figures should obviously be heading towards the hill, the other group should equally obviously be heading away from it.

The group about to attain the slopes of 'Happiness Hill' could include

Mr Sympathy, Miss Kindness, Mr Help, Mrs Forgiveness, Master Cheerful, Mr Contentment etc. Moving away from the hill could be Mrs Greed, Mr Envy, Master Selfishness, Miss Suspicion, Mr Jealousy etc.

Once this material has been prepared there is a great deal of scope for using it in several dramatic ways in the assembly presentation.

For example, remove the figures one at a time and bring them to the front of the presenting group. There might be a mime or a story telling how Miss Kindness, or whoever it is, got to 'Happiness Hill'. Similarly, stories and mimes could be produced to show why the undesirable characters failed to reach the hill.

One of the advantages of an assembly like this is that its appeal to very young children can be capitalised on in the classroom afterwards, and a great deal of useful, practical classroom RE can stem from it. The frieze, too, could be left in the hall in a conspicuous position so that its presence reminded passers-by of the story and its implications.

A7 Let there be light

The fact that Britain is increasingly becoming more of a multi-cultural society is a sound reason why all schools should have some assemblies that concern other cultures. Of course, in schools where there are many children of different cultures such services should be more frequent.

An ideal time of year to pursue a theme of 'Light', which involves other cultures, is in the dark days of November or December. One of the reasons for this is that three great festivals are celebrated in fairly close proximity at this time of the year. The Hindu celebration of Divali often falls in early November, whilst Hannukkah, the Jewish Festival of Lights, and the Christian celebration of St Lucia are both commemorated in December.

The class presenting the assembly could therefore use the common theme of 'Light' to link the three festivals. Each could be illustrated by an amalgam of words, actions and visual aids.

Divali is the Hindu New Year Festival. It celebrates the events that took place when Sita, the beautiful wife of Rama, King of India, was kidnapped by the evil King Ravana. For years Rama searched for her until he finally rescued her from Sri Lanka. Hindus remember this triumph of 'good' over 'evil' and 'light' over 'darkness' by lighting bonfires, burning effigies of Ravana, letting off fireworks and lighting up their homes. There is feasting and dancing and the exchange of presents. One group of presenters might mime the story of Rama and Sita to a reading; another might then re-enact a modern Hindu celebration of the event.

Hannukkah, the Jewish Festival of Lights, lasts for eight days and is a happy occasion which celebrates the time in AD 165 when the Jews freed their land from Antiochus Epiphanes. On each of the eight days fresh candles are lit, children play games and presents are exchanged. The presenting group might have prepared in advance a frieze depicting several features of this festival. This could be unrolled in the assembly and a reader might then draw attention to the special features on it.

St Lucia's day is on 13 December, and her festival appears to be celebrated in Sweden more fervently than anywhere else. One legend about this fourth-century saint suggests that she was blinded for refusing to renounce Christianity; another tells that she wore a crown of candles round her head to light her path and leave both of her hands free to carry provisions to hidden Christians. On December 13th young girls in Sweden dress in white, wear a crown of candles in their hair and lead processions round their communities. They distribute coffee and wheat cakes to people *en route* (should this be attempted, full safety precautions should be taken).

There is plenty of scope here for the presenting group to offer an interesting interpretation of this story.

Interwoven in this assembly could be the placing of various visual aids, which could be left behind for members of the school to look at in their own time. Included in these might be a calendar of great religious festivals from all cultures; some photographs of Hindus/Jews/Christians worshipping; one or two written quotations from various religions. Some taped or recorded music could also be used – Indian instrumental, Negro spiritual etc. These should instigate further interest in other classrooms.

Sources

For more details of Divali and Hannukkah, the appropriate chapter in this book could be consulted. The same applies for a calendar of religious festivals and some relevant quotations from various scriptures.

For those who want more detail concerning Hinduism and Judaism, *How People Worship*, by A.E. Perry, pub. Denholm House Press and E.J. Arnold (1974), is a useful little book.

Finally, for those who envisage a more substantial follow-up to this assembly, a thirty-minute film from the Education Department of Christian Aid (PO Box No. 1, London SW1W 9BW) could prove most useful. This film is called 'What do you mean by civilized?' and it was made with a multi-racial class in Tufnell Park Primary School, North London. The class acts a situation where an English and an African child exchange positions and cultures.

A8 Christmas

I have always been a great advocate of having parents in school when classes take assemblies. Children particularly enjoy this and it involves another group of people in the exercise of 'shared experience'. There is probably no time of the year when parents are more noticeable by their presence than at Christmas. They will obviously be in school if there is a 'production', their help with parties is always welcome, they delight in being involved with carol services and so on. Conversely, therefore, I would suggest that a Christmas assembly involving only those who actually work in the school would, on occasion, provide a vivid and thought-provoking change.

This might be particularly so if it was an assembly that allowed for cameo presentations from each class in turn, with the whole school being present to watch. Such an assembly need not take a great deal of preparation if a little co-operation and planning take into account what everybody is going to do, and the most effective order of presentation.

One suggestion here is to choose a theme based on the words: 'Christmas is a time for . . .'. Each class selects their theme to fill in the gap in this title. Such a service might develop as follows.

One class might decide that for them 'Christmas is a time for traditions.' Their presentation could then consist of readings, information, mimes, short plays, all built round the traditions of Christmas. Possible subjects for consideration here could include: candles, cards, Christingle, crackers, Christmas creatures, decorations, holly, light, Magi, manger, mistletoe, mummers, pantomimes, presents, robins, saints, star, shepherds, trees, wassail, yule.

Another class might concentrate on the theme that suggests that 'Christmas is a time for stories.' Included here could be the story of 'Silent Night' when the fact that mice had eaten the bellows of the church organ at Obendorf village meant that the priest and organist had to make up a new carol for the Christmas Eve service. They composed the guitar-accompanied carol to compensate for the lack of organ music. The story of Artaban, the fourth wise man, could be re-told. Late for his meeting with the other three wise men because he stopped to comfort a dying man, Artaban can never catch up with his colleagues because he constantly stops to help people in need and in doing so gives away the jewels he has brought as gifts for the new king. His final sacrifice is to give away his last jewel to stop soldiers killing one of the children who is to die as a result of Herod's edict to kill all babies in the hope of eliminating the threat of Jesus. The old Russian tale of Baboushka could be told. After acting as hostess to the three wise men she set off after them with her gift of black bread for the newly born infant. Because she cleaned her house before setting off she was too late to see the star and when she finally arrived at the stable Jesus was no longer there.

Other useful stories here could include a re-telling of the famous first world war incident when soldiers on opposite sides spontaneously crossed 'no-man's land' to join with each other in singing carols and celebrating Christmas; and one of the great traditionals like 'The little fir tree'.

A third class might select as their interpretation of the theme, 'Christmas is a time for celebration.' They might choose to do this through the medium of songs and food. A selection of carols could be sung which included old, new, possibly original examples from other countries. 'Food' might consider medieval and Victorian feasts, continental eating habits at this time of the year, and what the class has been cooking itself in school.

A fourth class might choose the unlikely title of 'Christmas is a time for writing' and then seek to intrigue the audience with some unusual and interesting examples of this. These could include some 'letters to Father Christmas', and this presents the opportunity to have some letters 'from Father Christmas', in the shape of some of the marvellous examples from Tolkien's book (*The Father Christmas Letters*, by J.R.R. Tolkien, pub. Allen and Unwin). There might also be letters of invitation, appreciation and thanks.

Another class might decide that 'Christmas is a time for looking'. They might consider and recount what is different about our local streets, our local churches and, indeed, our own school at this time of the year. Some members of the class might give simple demonstrations of craft work that they have produced to display in classroom or school.

A sixth aspect of the theme might come from a class that considers 'Christmas is a time for looking at the rest of the world.' Here we might learn more about the German 'Christkind', the French 'Père Noel' and the Dutch St Nicholas. The Swedish St Lucia celebrations could remind everyone of the girl saint who wore candles in her hair so that she could see the way through the dark caves to take food to renegade Christians. The spectacular Italian indoor decoration, the ceppo, could be described. In pyramid shape its combination of crib and Christmas tree contains pine cones, candles, fruit, presents and the group of figures representing the scene at the manger. We could learn more about the Mexican pinatas, decorated earthenware jars that are seen to contain presents when broken, and of the old Polish tradition whereby when children go to bed on Christmas Eve they lie on a covering of straw on their beds, in memory of Christ's birth.

A seventh presentation might be linked to 'Christmas is a time for giving.' Here a look might be taken at what presents are hoped for, how we can give to people without spending any money, what are the most precious gifts of all, how the school can, or is, giving to the local community and/or church, how the people in the school can give to each other.

The final part of this corporate service might be left to the youngest children. Their contribution might be one without words which portrays simply that 'Christmas is a time for remembering a birth.'

A9 Something different

Sometimes it is a very useful exercise to present an assembly that is completely different from the norm. One way of doing this is for the class responsible for the exercise to prepare all the visual and aural material beforehand. The assembly itself can then be presented by one or two children who manipulate the equipment, whilst the others who have contributed to the presentation can sit back with the audience and enjoy, and think about, the proceedings.

This sort of assembly could be done in two ways. The first could be to choose a story and ask the children to paint a series of pictures depicting this story. If these paintings are all the same size they could then be photographed to give 35mm colour transparencies. A 'sound track' of the story, with 'characters' speaking, and with appropriate sound effects could then be made. A rehearsal or two could then link the slides with the tape-recorded sounds.

A more sophisticated adaptation of this technique could involve the use of an overhead projector instead of slides. This time the best plan is to work out, and tape, the dialogue or sound effects first. When this has been done, the visual production can be planned. A series of scenes to fit the dialogue can be planned and the 'master' characters of the story drawn. These characters can then be traced onto a series of acetate sheets, ready for showing on the projector. The fact that the characters remain looking the same as the story progresses gives a touch of professionalism to the exercise and of course the scenes can be drawn round them as required.

The advantage of the overhead projector as opposed to a slide presentation is that it enables some animation to take place by movement of drawn shapes over the acetate sheet to give a superimposed effect. For those who get more expert at this exercise the next step is to use an acetate roll, instead of the sheets.

This time the scenes are drawn continuously on the roll which is timed to be turned in conjunction with the spoken commentary. The acetate roll is then fixed to the roller on the overhead projector and turned to the requirements of the 'sound track'. If used well, this type of equipment is extremely valuable for an unusual and very thought-provoking assembly.

In a presentation of this nature there are some very important practical points to remember. Only two or three children are needed to operate the various pieces of equipment on the morning of the presentation, but care is needed to be sure that all plugs are safe, a spare fuse or bulb is to hand if required, black-out is effective and that the audience can see properly. It is also true to say that the better the equipment the more likely it is to do justice to the children's efforts. For work of this nature I would thoroughly recommend the Goodsell PRCL Radio Cassette Recorder (12 watt), and the Portoscribe 700 overhead projector.

A10 Talents

One of the most satisfying of assemblies with young children is the presentation that reminds those with special talents of the need to share them, and encourages those who are apparently less gifted to see that there is almost always something an individual can contribute to the well-being of a group.

Such an assembly, based on a theme of 'Talents', could begin with the story of the Dürer brothers, one that always seems to have a great impact on children. Both Albert and Franz Dürer were talented artists. Lack of money prevented them studying together, so they arranged that one should work to support the other whilst he studied. The arrangement was that when one's studies were over they would exchange situations.

Franz, the elder brother, then supported Albert whilst the latter completed his studies. During this time Franz was employed on hard, physical labour. Eventually Albert's studies were complete but to his horror he then discovered that Franz's unselfish labouring work had so ruined his hands that he could now never hope to become a painter. As a tribute to his brother Albert painted what is probably his most famous picture – the praying hands. The hands shown are those of Franz, and the telling of the story obviously has greater impact if a reproduction of the painting can be shown. It is a fairly easy one to obtain and many copies were in circulation as a greeting card quite recently.

Having opened their assembly with this story, the presenting class might then switch to several groups each giving their interpretation of 'Talents'. The first group might present a 'talents of the class' compilation. Included in this could be poems, creative writing, paintings, drawings, tape recordings or actual performances of those who sing or play instruments well. For those children whose talents are not so easy to record, use of a simple camera might have resulted in photographs being available to show the rabbit hutch that Jimmy made at home, or the cake Mary made for her Gran's birthday etc.

This group could be followed by another dealing with 'the talents of the school'. Illustrations here might include such things as the cook's favourite recipe, a bookcase, shelving, decoration etc. which reflects the caretaker's skill, some typing by the secretary and so on. Choices of material here would obviously depend on the individual circumstances of each school.

A third group might present their findings on the 'talents of our town'. In this they could draw attention to skills and achievements of the people of the immediate locality. Included here could be builders, architects, housewives, local musicians, artists, drama groups, electricians, plumbers, examples of local industry etc. If some pre-assembly planning had included writing letters to people such as these, any replies received could add to the presentation. Personal contact and visitors to talk about their activities is of course an excellent follow-up activity here.

The fourth group might have a 'talents we hear about' collection. They could have examined newspapers for a week or two prior to the assembly to find inspiring stories similar to the one about the Dürers. These 'human interest' stories involving talents and skills could be read out.

The fifth group could end on a lively note with a theme of 'talents we enjoy'. Music is an obvious choice here, another is the rather outrageous poetry of someone like Spike Milligan, and a collection of cartoons is usually much enjoyed. Sport is another very large area that can be investigated.

The assembly might then be brought to a conclusion by posing a few questions to make everyone think: How do we get our talents? Can we afford to be conceited about them? Can we use them to help others? Do we use them enough?

Such questions could provoke thought about 'talents' like compassion, understanding, sympathy and tolerance. This could then allow the last word to be a Bible reading. Several verses in John 1 might be appropriate here and Luke 12: 15–21 could also be used.

Sources

For much of the material in this assembly 'local' sources of class, school and neighbourhood could be used. If something special in the way of a long, but deeply thought-provoking poem is wanted, 'Lord, I have time' by Michel Quoist, from *Prayers of Life*, pub. Gill and Macmillan, is an extremely powerful piece.

A11 The rhythm of life

Some assemblies can be prepared in general terms, with a specific section that can be adapted to meet the needs of a particular 'festive occasion' in the school year. Such an assembly could be built round this theme.

It could begin with an unusual and rhythmic introduction on record. Instead of the normal entry music, on this occasion some jazz could be used. This should be genuine, and a good choice could be made from New Orleans sources such as: 'New Orleans Function'; 'Just a Closer Walk with Thee'; 'Tin Roof Blues'. For those teachers who prefer to link music more explicitly with assembly proceedings, a possible compromise here would be one of the tracks from the collection of up tempo spirituals by the Golden Gate Quartet on 'Get On Board' (Columbia 335X 1370).

With the conclusion of the introductory music, everyone should be in position and the presenters could move straight into their routine.

SPEAKER 1   We are surrounded by rhythm
SPEAKER 2   Listen to our names.

An arrangement of the class's names could then be called out. The calling could be supplemented by a drum beat matching the syllables. (See illustration.)

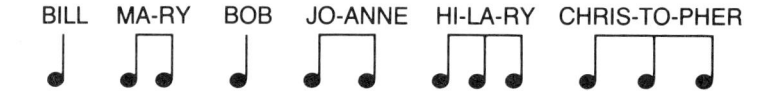

BILL   MA-RY   BOB   JO-ANNE   HI-LA-RY   CHRIS-TO-PHER

This noting of the rhythm of everyday school life could be further illustrated by nursery rhymes, playground games, multiplication tables and simple percussion work.

Following this introduction the presenters could go on to look at the rhythm of things on a larger scale. By means of a series of paintings, drawings and natural phenomena, if the time of year is right, the rhythm of the seasons could be shown. This could be followed by a look at the rhythm of our lives – breakfast, to school, lunchtime, school, home, the evening and its activities, bed, and then back to the beginning again.

This would seem a good point to sing a hymn. A good choice would be one characterised by a strong rhythm and with appropriate words. A well-known choice here could therefore be: 'He's got the whole world in His hands.'

Once again the singing of a hymn could provide a natural break to change the emphasis of the assembly. This time the course of events following the hymn would be determined by the time of the school year. The theme of rhythm could on this occasion be linked to 'celebration'.

Prior to celebration there is a time of thought and preparation, e.g.: Advent – Christmas; pre-Lenten activities – Lent – Easter.

These Christian celebrations could depend on the time of year. Other alternatives would be the linking of celebrations of different cultures, e.g.: Divali, Hannukkah, St Lucia's Day – a pattern or rhythm associated with 'Light'. Thus this part of the assembly could be adapted to suit almost any particular part of the year, and its position in the rhythm of celebration.

Regardless of the celebration or religion used in this part of the service a choice from the 'Thoughts and Prayers' section of this book should provide a suitable selection for the conclusion of the service.

Sources

'He's got the whole world in His hands' is in *Come and Praise*, BBC publications.
Festive Occasions in the Primary School, by Redvers Brandling, pub. Ward Lock Educational, contains material on 'celebrations'.

A12 Easter (1)

Easter remains perhaps the biggest dilemma that the primary school teacher has to face when dealing with assemblies and religious education. Here is one of the two most important events in the Christian year yet what happened in Jerusalem is so complex that most teachers feel it is well beyond the understanding of children under eleven years old.

This, then, is the crux of the problem. Do we ignore Easter, or do we move uneasily through a traditional telling of the story? I feel that one way in which this problem might be approached is to try and build up a factual background, in front of which a representation of some of the emotions and intrigue involved can be shown. This may not bring the child much nearer to understanding Easter but it could at least result in a recognition that this part of the Christian story is crucially important.

To consider this in practical terms, I think it is basically a top junior project which could be presented to the rest of the school by means of unconventional assemblies. Just how this is done will depend on individual situations, but it might be helpful to consider two lines of approach.

The first of these involves the main body of children being witness to a 'plot'. The scene could be set by one placard which announced: 'Jerusalem – nearly 2,000 years ago'. In front of this placard a group could hold a conversation that might evolve as follows:

A   I've been sent here to discuss how we might trap this fellow Jesus Christ.
B   Yes, one of our council told me that he would be in Jerusalem for the Passover Feast.
C   It's going to be difficult to try and capture him in the city with all those people here, though.
A   Mmmmm. I wondered if we could let it be known that there might be a reward for anybody who gives information leading to this man's capture.
B   That's not a bad idea. Look you'd better start spreading the word round about that.
A   Yes, but we still need to know where this Jesus Christ and his followers will be when they are inside the city. The only way to do that is to have them followed all the time.
C   Right, well if we draw a map in the dust here we can decide where we are going to plant our men to do their watching.
(Map 'drawn' by plotters in the dust on the floor)
B   Well we're going to need a man at the Temple and another here at the Pool of Siloam.

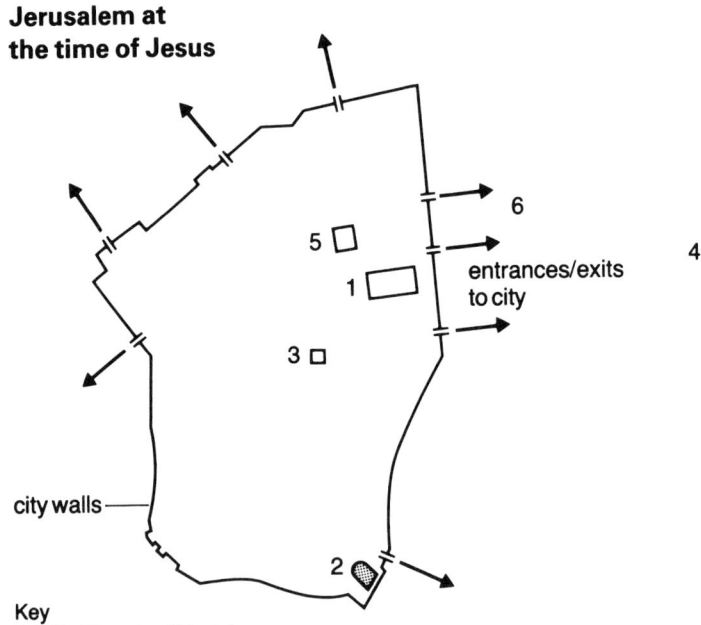

Jerusalem at the time of Jesus

city walls

entrances/exits to city

Key
1 The Temple of Herod
2 Pool of Siloam – where Jesus healed a blind man
3 Forum – Roman theatre
4 Mount of Olives
5 Antonia Fortress – home of Pontius Pilate
6 Garden of Gethsemane

A Yes, and there'd better be somebody at the Forum, and somebody near the Mount of Olives.
C Better have somebody at the Antonia Fortress too.
A Mmmmm. Then we'll have him watched from the moment he enters the city gates.
B But what do we do after that? What do the Sanhedrin want to do when he is captured?
A (*smiling*) Oh we don't have to worry then. They've got a long list of charges: causing disturbances, practising medicine without a licence, associating with criminals, behaviour likely to cause a riot. And there's plenty more.

The enactment of a scene such as the one described here should certainly provoke a great deal of thought, and at its conclusion some further visual and aural material could be used to add to the atmosphere. The 'map drawn on the floor' could be ready in the wings on a piece of large card. It could then be produced and held up for all to see. See the plan for an idea of what it might look like.

Pre-assembly planning could have included making up a 'Wanted poster' such as the protagonists in the plot suggest should be circulated round the city. The American-based Jesus Movement distributed a poster like this in their campaigning a few years ago and copies of this might still be in existence. One made by the children could consider the things mentioned in the conversation. It might look something like the example shown.

```
┌─o─────────────────────────────────────o─┐
│            REWARD                        │
│  For information leading to the capture of Jesus Christ - │
│    alias The Messiah, King of Kings, Son of God.          │
│   This man is guilty of many offences against religion    │
│                  and the state.                           │
│         Can you help in his capture?                      │
└─o─────────────────────────────────────o─┘
```

Further information could be written out and displayed in connection with such things as the Jewish Council of the Sanhedrin and the Passover Feast. The sound background could be stimulated by using Rimsky-Korsakov's 'Russian Easter Overture' Op. 36.

With this assembly a certain atmosphere should have been created. There should be suspense, anticipation and queries. Why do these people want to capture Jesus? What has he really done? Are they frightened of him? This combination of features should then set the scene for a second assembly on the subject.

A13 Easter (2)

The second assembly related to Easter would follow on naturally from the scene set with Easter (1). How this second assembly might be presented could be a matter of choice. The theme this time would be the 'interviewing' of several people who could give 'first hand comments' on what happened in Jerusalem.

This might be prepared entirely in a classroom so that the final product was presented in assembly as a well-amplified tape recorded 'radio interview'. An alternative would be to stage a presentation where the 'interviewer' is stationed at the front of the hall with a telephone. Explaining to the audience who he is about to ring, he telephones a variety of people from the past who answer his questions. The children answering the questions could be screened off and the use of a microphone with a machine such as the Goodsell radio/cassette recorder would give their voices an unusual effect, be an aid to clarity, and increase the atmosphere of the proceedings. The children who are screened off could use scripts to read their replies, but, obviously, careful rehearsal would be needed to ensure what sounded like spontaneity, and to eliminate practical details like rustling papers etc.

The suggestions that follow are based on this type of presentation.

The interviewer could first explain to the audience exactly what is about to happen.

INTERVIEWER Good morning, ladies and gentlemen. As you see, here I have a telephone. But this is no ordinary phone. By dialling a certain secret number I can phone people of the past. Waiting to speak to me at the other end of this line are some of these people. The first of them is one of the crowd who saw Jesus enter Jerusalem on that triumphant day in about AD 30. I'm going to call now.

(*Interviewer dials, waits for phone to be answered. Speaks*)

INT. Good morning. Is that Ahmed? I'm speaking from – school as we arranged. Can you tell us something about that day when Jesus entered Jerusalem?

(*Amplified reply now heard*)

AHMED Certainly, certainly. Oh it was a great day. Lots of Jesus' friends had come up from Galilee. They had gone into Jerusalem before him and told people there that he was about to enter the city. There was a great feeling of enthusiasm.

INT. What happened next?

AHMED Well, in the distance everybody saw Jesus approaching on a donkey. They then cut down branches from nearby palm trees and spread them on the ground leading into the city.

INT. Were the crowd cheering?

AHMED   Oh yes – cheering, shouting, singing. There was a great cry of 'Hosannah, Hosannah in the Highest'.

INT.   Do you think any of Jesus' enemies were in the crowd?

AHMED   No doubt about that – but the last thing they wanted was a disturbance on the streets. They just kept in the background.

INT.   Thank you Ahmed. Would you put Zachariah on the line now please?

ZACHARIAH   Zachariah here.

INT.   Good morning Zachariah. I believe you could tell us something about how the plot against Jesus developed.

ZACH.   Yes indeed. I was a servant working for Jesus' enemies you see – and they could hardly believe their luck when this man Judas turned up.

INT.   Could you explain?

ZACH.   Well, as Ahmed said, these were Jews and they were frightened of what would happen if there was a disturbance on the streets and the Romans had to interfere. They wanted to capture Jesus and then present him as a criminal. Judas gave them their chance.

INT.   How was that?

ZACH.   He told them where Jesus would be that night. He also said he would go up to Jesus and greet him so that the soldiers would know exactly who to arrest.

INT.   Why did he do this?

ZACH.   Money came into it – there were thirty pieces of silver in it for him. I understand afterwards he was so ashamed that he tried to give the money back, and eventually he killed himself.

INT.   Is the Roman soldier there, Zachariah?

ZACH.   Yes, I'm putting him on now.

INT.   Thank you – Augustus? I believe you can tell us something about what happened in the Garden of Gethsemane.

AUGUSTUS   I can. We got orders to go out beyond the city walls late at night to this Garden of Gethsemane. There we were supposed to arrest a trouble-maker who was said to be stirring up some sort of revolution.

INT.   How did you know which was he?

AUG.   Ah – one of his so-called friends was to go up to him and greet him. Then we had to move in quickly and arrest this Jesus.

INT.   What happened?

AUG.   We got out there – spotted the man and moved in. There was a bit of a skirmish but nothing much. Those who called themselves disciples ran away. We tied Jesus' arms and took him to the house of the High Priest, Caiaphas, for questioning.

INT.   Thank you, Augustus.

(*Then holding hand over telephone mouthpiece, Interviewer speaks to audience.*)

INT. We know that Jesus was questioned by Caiaphas and a message was sent to the Roman governor, Pontius Pilate, asking him to hold a special court the next morning. But our next speaker can tell us something about what happened to the disciples.

(*He then turns back to the phone and speaks into it.*)

INT. Joan, could you tell us about the night of the arrest?

JOAN Yes, of course. I remember the night well. I'd been one of the crowd who had cheered Jesus' entry into the city and I particularly remembered one of his disciples – a big, strong-looking chap.

INT. Did you see this man after Jesus had been arrested?

JOAN Oh yes. There were several of us round a warm fire near the High Priest's house when this man came up. I even knew his name was Peter.

INT. What happened?

JOAN I said to him – you're one of the Messiah's friends aren't you? 'No,' he replied, quick as a flash. I asked him again and he still said no. Well I didn't see him for a bit after that and then, when it was almost dawn, I went up to him again and said, "You're Peter – I know you are." When he said he wasn't again, a cock suddenly crowed. He then went deathly pale, covered his face with his hands and dashed off.

INT. Thank you Joan. I'd like to speak to Pontius Pilate now please. Can you send a message?

PILATE This is Pontius Pilate.

INT. Sir, could you tell us what events took place on the morning that Jesus was brought before you in Jerusalem?

PILATE I remember it well. As Roman governor, all I wanted was peace in the city. This Jesus didn't seem to have done anything wrong, as far as I could see, but he obviously had enemies. When I said I would release him because of the Passover celebration the crowd went wild. 'Crucify him' was all they would shout. Finally I decided I could find no guilt with him so I sent for a bowl of water. In front of the crowd I washed my hands and told the enemies of this man I was having nothing more to do with his case.

INT. Thank you.

(*Puts down the telephone and speaks to the audience*)

INT. So ladies and gentlemen, we have heard how some of the events looked to people who were in Jerusalem all those years ago. I wonder what your opinions are? Who was right? Would you have acted differently, and if so, how?

At this point the assembly could be concluded, leaving many points open for further discussion and consideration in the more intimate atmosphere of the various classrooms.

Sources

For those wishing to use Bible sources in connection with the Easter story, appropriate refs. are: Matthew 26, 27; Mark 14–16; Luke 22, 23; John 18, 19.

An excellent book for reference here is *The Book of the Bible – an Encyclopedic Guide to the World's greatest Book*, pub. Purnell.

A14   What's in a name?

Some assembly themes, once chosen, result in such a mass of material being gathered that there is the danger of overwhelming the audience with detail. One way of avoiding this is to select the material best-suited to a thoughtful and dramatic presentation, and leave other information in a prominent place to inspire follow-up work in various classrooms.

'What's in a name?' is the sort of theme that can be approached from several angles, but one of the best starting points with young children would seem to be through their own names. The service might begin with the presenters reciting the old rhyme:

> What's your name?
> Mary Jane.
> Where do you live?
> Down the lane.
> What do you keep?
> A little shop.
> What do you sell?
> Ginger pop
> How many bottles do you sell in a day?
> Twenty-four, now go away.

From this starting point various speakers from the presenters might give information about common surnames, e.g. the first 'Smiths' were people who 'smote' metal into useful shapes, and now one person in every thirty-seven in the British Isles is called Smith; 'Wright' is a name that came from people who 'wrought' wood; 'Robinson' came about through a boy being named after his father – Robin's son; 'Little' or 'Small' stems from the fact that people who bear this name now probably had ancestors of short stature; 'Armstrong' originated from a man noted for his strength.

Following this, the presentation could move on to consider how all objects have names. In this context the presenters might concentrate on the strange names we find in a church. Two of the group could, at this stage, pin on to a display board the following list: font, pulpit, aisle, organ, porch, altar, steeple, gargoyles, arches, nave, chancel, tombs.

Each word could be spoken as it is pinned up but no more information given. When this has been done a speaker could say that all these words are connected with the Christian Church, but that there are other religions that have special names for things too. In conjunction with these comments another list could be displayed: Koran, Mosque, Synagogue, Torah. These words, too, could be left without comment.

By this time in the assembly a hymn involving the participation of all would be refreshing. Possible choices here might be: 'What is your name?'; 'For all the strength'; 'We need each other whoever we are'.

Once the hymn is over the assembly could move into its second half by taking a slightly different approach. This time a look could be taken at other names. A start might be made with 'Saint' and the stories of one or two saints could be told to illustrate this. Other possible choices, or alternatives, here might include 'Famous names' (Mother Theresa, Florence Nightingale, Dr Barnardo etc.): 'Names we would like to be called' (hero, friend, saviour); 'Names we would not like to be called' (fool, thief, traitor); 'Names with special meanings' (victim, martyr, missionary, pilgrim, prophet, disciple).

Obviously, careful selection would be needed here if these various names were to be illustrated by a story or mime related to them. The opportunity of displaying them all somewhere should, however, not be neglected. Once this stage of the assembly has been reached, instead of the normal thoughts or prayers, a selection of famous and thought-provoking sayings emanating from various religions and suitable for (or adapted to be suitable for) the age-group concerned could be used. Gandhi's comment that: 'I am a Muslim, a Sikh, a Christian and a Jew' is an example here of a statement that could be used to provoke more thought and discussion later. Other selections could be made from the 'Thoughts and Prayers' section of this book.

The assembly could then be concluded, but many of the items that have been mentioned, but not elaborated on, would provide stimuli for follow-up work in classrooms. For instance, the various displays of names should be left in a prominent position, and one section of these might encourage a visit to a local church. Others could provide for much valid research in the school library.

Sources

The three hymns mentioned can all be found in *New Orbit*, pub. Galliard. *On Location – Churches*, by Henry Pluckrose, pub. Mills and Boon is a useful book for following up church visits.

A15 **Building a life**

The teacher who regularly prepares an assembly with a group of children rapidly becomes aware of the advantage of adapting a wide variety of material. An excellent example of this can be seen from an assembly centred on the theme of 'Building'.

In the primary school, and particularly at the lower end of it, a great deal of time is spent trying to guide children into the awareness of a 'person'. This includes, ultimately, not only awareness of themselves but also an appreciation of the needs, feelings, emotions and weaknesses of others. From this gradual acquisition of awareness and knowledge come opportunities for practical concern and lessons learnt by example.

It is this sort of pre-assembly aim that could result in an assembly starting with the children entering the hall to the sound of a record containing 'The Building Song'. This is on BBC Record No. 147S, 'Get Together' and the song in question has a lively tune and words that suggest how people must build their lives, in different ways, all over the world. At the end of the song, and with everybody settled in the hall, the presenting group could then develop the theme of 'Building'.

Advance preparation might have one group ready with a few bricks, hods, shovels and cement-bags to hand. This group could then act or mime that the construction of a building was something that needed careful planning and application. Ample illustration could be drawn from shovels for foundations, bricks for soundness and so on.

This process could then be compared with the similar need to 'build a life'. It could be asked what 'materials' are needed here. This time it could be suggested that satisfactory lives are built from combinations of love and care from parents and friends; awareness of others and consideration for them; contact with other people; a sense of purpose. Obviously, these ideas would need to be expressed in language appropriate to the presenters and their audience.

Perhaps the next facet of the assembly would be to show that whilst everybody tries to 'build their own lives' they do this in a variety of different ways, circumstances and countries. To support this idea a group of the presenters might show some paintings of their own of children in other parts of the world. Whilst this is being done another band of 'Get Together' might be played. This is the song 'Wonderful World', and James Thiem's words are very relevant to this assembly theme. A typical, thought-provoking example is: 'Take care to wonder at the world through which you wander.'

The next step might be to remind everybody that we learn so much in life by studying the lives of other people. Some 'inspiring' examples might then be given and this would seem a good opportunity to use some of the simply-told but evocative stories from Alan Dale's *New World*.

Similarly, some illustrations from secular literature could also be included. Two suggestions here might be *Carrie's War*, by Nina Bawden and *The House of Sixty Fathers*, by Meidert De Jong. Contained in this pair of Puffins are passages showing the fears and difficulties of life for the handicapped Johnny, and the joy of being re-united with one's parents after a long and enforced absence.

One of the best qualities of an assembly such as this is the fact that it offers so many follow-up possibilities. The imaginative teacher could suggest a number of situations and consequences back in the classroom and invite the children to discuss how they would react to them. These would help to emphasise that 'building a life' is a very difficult thing to do well.

Sources

'Get Together', BBC Record 147S
New World – the heart of the New Testament in Plain English, by Alan Dale, pub. OUP.
Carrie's War, by Nina Bawden, pub. Puffin.
The House of Sixty Fathers, by Meidert De Jong, pub. Puffin.

A16 Never judge a book . . .

To look beyond the surface of people and situations is an excellent means of exploring some very important facets of life. To use this theme in a class assembly presentation allows for the use of a variety of interesting and thought-provoking material.

The assembly might begin by one child saying the first half of this idiom: 'Never judge a book . . .'

A second child might then add: '. . . by its cover',

A third speaker could then say that by the end of the assembly everybody would understand much more clearly what this meant. The first example illustrating the saying could be a short play based upon St Matthew, chapter 21, verses 28–31. This could develop as follows:

FARMER (*to his two sons*) Well, boys, I've got a great deal to do on the farm tomorrow and I would like you both to help me.
JOHN Certainly Dad, I don't mind at all. I'll be down at the barn ready to start promptly at nine o'clock.
PETER I've got a lot of my own work to do tomorrow, Dad. I don't know that I can manage to help, but I'll try.
(*Outside the barn, next day.*)
FARMER Quarter past nine and no sign of either of them . . . ah, somebody is coming.

PETER   Hello, Dad. I stayed in all last night and got my own work finished, so I'm free to help you today. I got here as soon as I could.
FARMER   Thanks, Peter. I'm glad you could come, but John promised that he would be here promptly at nine o'clock.
READER   The farmer and Peter waited for another half an hour but John did not turn up. Peter and his father worked in the fields all day. John did not come at all.

Further illustrations could then follow from the children to show that we need to get to know people before we can judge them properly. These illustrations might include Quasimodo in Hugo's *The Hunchback of Notre Dame*, who, because he was so ugly, was considered devoid of human feelings. Viewed from the other end of the spectrum could be Marilla, the well known character in L.M. Montgomery's *Ann of Avonlea*. Here we have a surface appearance of prim, proper authority, but underneath there is the traditional 'heart of gold'. Further references might include instances of good deeds that have been reported in local papers.

This theme could then be developed further to show that some people want to be helpful and kind but are stopped by characteristics like shyness, loneliness, guilt, fear of embarrassment and so forth. A further illustration from the Bible provides another object lesson here. This is the story of Zaccheus, Luke 19: 1–10.

At this point in the assembly the presenters might sing a hymn that they have learned specially for the occasion. An excellent choice here would be 'People' which is by J. Naylor and can be found in the most useful anthology, *New Orbit*. The words of this 'hymn', are in fact only four lines long, with suggestions to users to extend it with their own words. The words given fit in exactly with the theme of this assembly, e.g.:

> Oh people are fat and people are thin,
> And all goodness and gentleness comes from within.

The five bar tune is easily mastered so there is scope here for some 'instant learning'. The presenters could deliver four verses and then, with only a little help, the rest of the school should be capable of joining in a re-singing of these verses.

The service might then be concluded by a display of questions and statements held up on large sheets of paper or card. Whilst these are in position other children amongst the presenters could read out a series of prayers, thoughts and appropriate passages. Some of these might be taken from the 'Thoughts and Prayers' section of this book. The questions or statements posed in the display might include: 'Is appearance important?'; 'Actions speak louder than words'. 'Don't make promises you can't keep'; 'Do you behave to others as you would like them to behave to you?'

84 Class Assemblies

I hope these comments would be only the starting point for some closer inspection of the issues in various classrooms afterwards.

Sources

New Orbit – songs and hymns for under elevens, editor, Peter Smith, pub. Galliard.

A17 Partnerships

A class assembly based on the theme of 'Partnerships' could be presented as the work of groups of children. The progression of the service might be as follows.

The entry music of the presenting group might be 'The Wedding March'. Once the children were in position two readers could set the scene with their opening comments.

READER 1 Our assembly this morning is about partnerships.
READER 2 We are going to look at some of the things needed to make a good partnership.
READER 1 Listen again to the music that began our assembly. It is called 'The Wedding March'.

As the music begins again, the first group of children could move into position to present their consideration of a partnership, such as marriage. Some of the children could then mime the progress of a wedding service. This could be guided by a spoken commentary, with appropriate pauses for the children to take the relevant action. The commentary could be done by the teacher 'off stage', one of the class's more capable readers, or a tape prepared before the assembly. It might include the following:

'Different religions have different customs at their marriage services. They are all very important ceremonies for the two people who are getting married. At a Christian marriage service the bride will be trying to look her very best and will probably wear a beautiful, long white dress. She will have some bridesmaids in beautiful dresses too, and they will have bouquets of flowers. The bride's family and friends will sit on the left-hand side of the church.

'The bridegroom's family will sit on the right-hand side of the church, and a friend of the bridegroom's, who is known as the best man, will be sitting in one of the front seats.

'The bride's father brings her to the church and walks with his daughter down the aisle of the church whilst "The Wedding March" is being played. When they reach the front of the church, the bridegroom and the best man join the bride. The priest then stands in front of the couple who are going to be married. He asks the people there if anyone knows any reason why these two people should not be married. If there is no answer, he continues with the service. The best man hands the bridegroom the wedding ring and the groom puts it on the bride's finger. The wedding is sealed with the words, "I give you this ring as a sign of our marriage . . ." and the priest says, "I proclaim that they are husband and wife." When the service is finished the newly married couple and their attendants go into the vestry of the church. There they sign the register showing the details and date of the marriage.'

As this commentary is being spoken the miming group should have depicted its various aspects. At the conclusion the two speakers could present themselves to the audience again.

SPEAKER 1   Marriage is a partnership.
SPEAKER 2   It needs many qualities to make it work properly. Trust, reliability . . .
SPEAKER 1   Wait, wait. We want to look at some other partnerships first.

This could provide the cue for the next group to present its findings. These might be based on a theme of partnerships where friends help each other. Consideration might be given here to the partnership of man and animal in the case of a blind person and a guide dog, and for the relationship between friends there is an enormous amount of material to choose from. Those who wish to use Bible sources might refer to the story of David and Jonathan. Among more modern examples there is the climber Edmund Hillary who, despite three broken ribs and many difficulties with an ice overhang in a crevasse, still hauled his friend Jim McFarlane to safety after the latter had fallen in the crevasse.

At this stage in the service the audience might be invited to join in and sing a hymn appropriate to the development of the assembly so far, to prepare for the final part. Such a hymn might be: 'The Family of Love', (page 100).

When the hymn is finished the last part of the service could consider the partnership of 'Christian and Cross', or man and his beliefs. This, of course, would have to be done in a manner and in language appropriate to the age group. One starting point here could be a display of three crosses. One of these could be the road sign for crossroads. (See illustration.)

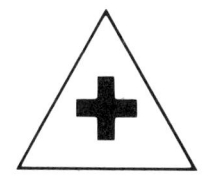

red triangle
white background
black cross

The second could be the red cross on the white background, depicting the Red Cross organisation; the third could be a picture of the Victoria Cross. (See illustration.)

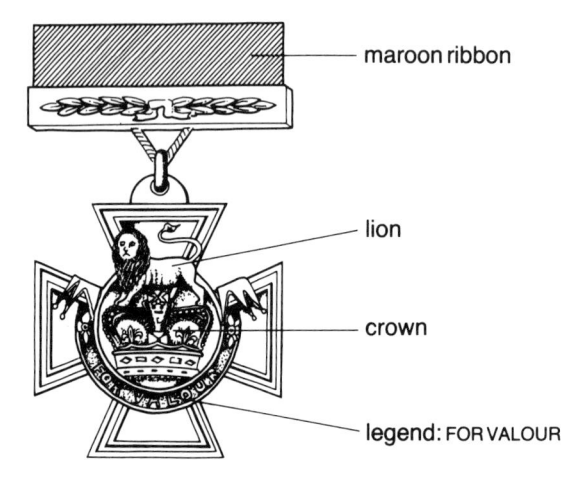

Diagram of Victoria Cross with labels: maroon ribbon, lion, crown, legend: FOR VALOUR

As these are held up, they could form the basis of the words to end the assembly:

'Looking at these crosses helps us to remember some of the things that are so important to successful partnerships. A crossroads means that the person approaching them must make a decision about which way to go. In all partnerships we have to make decisions to give our trust and loyalty. The Red Cross reminds us that in a partnership we may often have to give sympathy and real help when it is needed. The Victoria Cross reminds us that we must have the courage to be unselfish and think of others and not ourselves.'

With these words the assembly could be concluded and a different record might be used to sustain thought on the theme as the children leave the hall. Possibilities here could include: 'The Bridal Chorus' from Lohengrin or the 'Romeo and Juliet' overture.

A18 Guidance

Assemblies taken by groups of children can make an impact in a number of different ways. One of the most significant is to begin with a combination of the visual and the unusual. Here is an intriguing start to an assembly with the overall theme of guidance.

Once the audience is in place in the hall the presenters could enter in the following way. At first only three would make their appearance, each carrying a large piece of card or paper on which sea marking buoys are painted. These paintings would represent the illustrated buoys. Each child carrying a painting could then stand in a space near the presenting area in the hall, and between them they could call out the significant information:

SPEAKER 1   Our class is soon coming into harbour to present our assembly.
SPEAKER 2   We are here to see that they are safely guided into harbour.
SPEAKER 3   Watch how they come in. If they were all on a ship, the ship would have to keep the Conical buoy on its right (or starboard) side as it entered harbour.
SPEAKER 1   The Can buoy would be kept on its left (or port) side.
SPEAKER 2   The Spherical buoy marks a shallow patch but can be passed on either side.

As these comments are concluded the rest of the class could enter the hall circuiting the buoys in the manner described. Once they are in position the service could continue with a hymn with a nautical flavour – 'For those in peril on the sea'; 'The sun that shines across the sea'; 'Fisherman Peter on the sea'.

Following the hymn, some of the children could then make comments to focus attention on the real essentials of the assembly:

SPEAKER 1   If we had been on a ship we would have needed guidance from the buoys.
SPEAKER 2   As human beings, we all need guidance in our lives.
SPEAKER 3   (*turning to the rest of the presenters*) Who gives us guidance?

At this point a question and answer response could be most effective, with answers to Speaker 3's question, such as parents, teachers, friends, relatives.

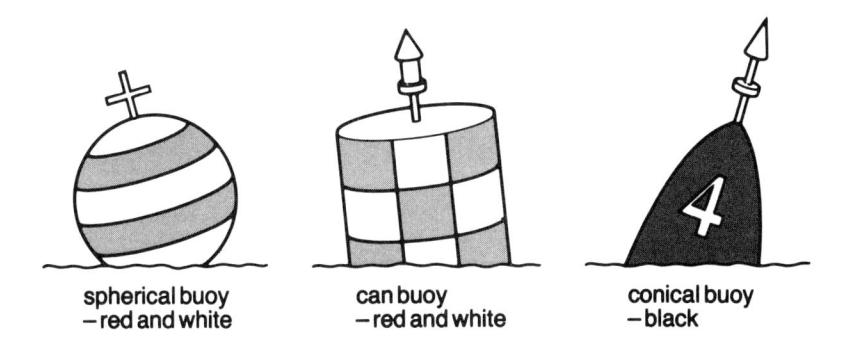

spherical buoy
– red and white

can buoy
– red and white

conical buoy
– black

At the conclusion of this feature the point could be made that many people find guidance by being very quiet and thinking deeply about decisions they have to make. Churches are quiet places where people go to think in surroundings of beauty and peace. This stage of the service is an ideal time to include some prayers or thoughts for all to share.

Following the prayers the assembly could be concluded with a short and simple play. This can be presented without any moralising at its conclusion, the sentiments that it expresses being in themselves sufficient food for thought and discussion when the audience return to their classrooms.

The play could evolve as follows. A narrator might stand to one side of the proceedings, while an 'old man' takes up position by a 'road side'.

NARRATOR   One day a wise old man sat alongside the road leading into his town. A stranger approached.

STRANGER   Hello there – I am on my way to London. (*Substitute the name of the local town or village here.*) Can you tell me what the people are like there?

OLD MAN   What are the people like in the town you have come from?

STRANGER   Oh they are mean, selfish, hard to get on with and unpleasant.

OLD MAN   You'll find them just the same in London, then.

NARRATOR   The stranger went on his way, to be followed shortly afterwards by another whom the old man had never seen before.

2ND STRANGER   Good morning. I'm on my way to London. Tell me, what are the people like there?

OLD MAN   What are they like in the town you have come from?

2ND STRANGER   Well, they're kind and helpful and usually very generous.

OLD MAN   You'll find them just the same in London, then.

Sources

For the hymns contained in this assembly, 'For those in peril on the sea' can be found in many traditional hymn books.

'The sun that shines across the sea' is in *Someone's Singing Lord*, pub. A. and C. Black.

'Fisherman Peter on the sea' is in *New Orbit*, pub. Galliard.

A19 Self help

The avowed aim of many of the charitable organisations serving Third World countries is that help provided should ultimately lead to people being able to help themselves, by learning new skills, operating equipment etc. This idea of 'self help' is a useful one to pursue in an assembly.

Bearing in mind that a good assembly is rather like a good short story in its need for an arresting opening, gradual progression and satisfying dénouement, the beginning of such an assembly might be as follows.

Once the audience are in place the presenters could appear to be about to start their service, but an aura of self-doubt and lack of preparation should be allowed to show. This atmosphere of unpreparedness, 'who speaks first, what do I say, you should come in now', will quickly transmit itself to the watching children. As schools in which children regularly take assembly will be used to efficiency and good organisation (one hopes!) this contrast would be most noticeable and unusual.

The teacher in charge will have been able to calculate at exactly what point this apparent inefficiency can be exposed for what it is – apparent inefficiency only. She will then stop proceedings and explain. The class could then go on to elaborate on how important it is to prepare things properly.

At this point they might produce some photographs of Third World situations in which help is obviously needed. Readings and comments linked with these could explain that help in such situations is often 'preparation'. That is to say, money collected aims at combating problems on a long term basis – giving a tractor as well as immediate food supplies; investigating irrigation problems to aid crop growth; building schools as well as hospitals.

At this stage in the service a hymn epitomising 'self help' could be sung. This is Cecily Taylor's 'The Hungry Man'. The theme of this hymn complements the philosophy of the assembly in that it emphasises how help given is most beneficial if, when dealing with the recipient, it can in 'many lasting ways . . . help his future days'.

Following the hymn the assembly could continue to show the importance of preparedness and self help by giving illustrations in story and mime. Biblical references that might be used here include those of the girls without oil for their lamps at the wedding feast (Matthew 25; 1–11), and the story of the house built on inadequate foundations (Matthew 7; 24–7). A possibility for miming could be based on Benjamin Franklin's tale of Richard III's lack of preparation when:

> For want of a nail a shoe was lost
> For want of a shoe a horse was lost
> For want of a horse a rider was lost
> For want of a rider a battle was lost
> For want of a battle a kingdom was lost
> And all for want of a horseshoe nail.

Then, moving right back to the children's immediate environment, attention could be drawn to the fact that by doing our best at school we are preparing ourselves to be more useful people to both ourselves and others. Our lessons help us to become more knowledgeable about the world; our contact with other children and teachers helps us to understand the need for tolerance and sympathy when living with others; our good fortune in receiving so many of the benefits of modern living should help us to understand the needs of those less fortunate than ourselves, and perhaps be able to do something to help them.

This would seem an ideal moment for all to pause for some thoughts and prayers. Some of the following words might be used:

'Let us think this morning about preparing ourselves to live useful lives in which we may be of help to other people. Let us try to learn from our mistakes; to benefit from our opportunities; to help ourselves by using time well and not wasting it. Let us try to have courage to face disappointments; patience to overcome difficulties; energy to help others. Let us think about helping ourselves to gain the sort of qualities that we admire in others'.

Following the prayers, the assembly could end with everyone departing to the music and words of 'The Hungry Man' again – but this time on record.

Sources

'The Hungry Man', by Cecily Taylor: words and music in *New Orbit*, pub. Galliard; on record Avant Garde AV 131.
Third World photographs and other useful assembly material from Christian Aid (PO Box No. 1, London SW1W 9BW).

Music and Assembly

Most primary schools have a very limited repertoire of hymns and it is hoped that the six included here will prove of the type that children of this age enjoy singing. I have found this to be so, and none of these hymns is difficult to learn.

In the rest of the section the emphasis is on suggestions that will encourage children's musical participation in assemblies.

On occasions when I have been involved with teachers' courses on Assembly, one question can almost always be guaranteed: 'What about music for assembly?' People's taste in music differs widely but all seem concerned with three major issues:

(a) What records are useful for introductory/background/scene setting music?
(b) Which hymn books could be recommended?
(c) What part can children play as musicians in assemblies?

With regard to (a), personal choice and availability are two very important factors, but it is possible to be guided by one or two general rules. For a start, it might be useful to build up a small record collection which could be broadly categorised under four headings: Classical; Religious/Folk; Sound Effects; Jazz.

Selections of classical music provide a wide variety of 'entry' music. 'Scheherezade', 'Swan Lake', 'Liebestraum' are the sort of pieces useful for establishing a tranquil atmosphere; marches such as the 'Radetzky', 'Grand March from Aïda' and Tchaikovsky's 'Marche Slave' set a more vigourous tone; Wagner's 'Flying Dutchman' overture, Mussorgsky's 'Night on the Bare Mountain' imply fear and disturbance; a selection of waltzes from Gounod, Strauss, Weber and Tchaikovsky could make a light-hearted beginning. Thus individual selections of classical records are well worth collecting because their evocative short passages can be used in a variety of contexts.

Religious/Folk records in assemblies often present songs with words containing a 'message' set in the sort of rhythmic accompaniment that children enjoy listening to. The BBC produce some excellent records here. There is a selection listed in 'Sources' below, but for a good example, the Crown Folk singing 'Let Loose', a version of the Good Samaritan with a compulsive sung chorus, would be hard to beat.

A couple of good sound-effects records are invaluable in any school collection. These are very useful for backing up mimes in assembly; for providing appropriate noises to a slide presentation; as sound effects supplementing a story. My choice here is again from the BBC. Record RED 106M contains sounds like: village atmosphere, urban morning, industry, public transport, park etc., whilst 'Out of this World' BBC REC 225, moves into the more exotic fields of dreaming, uncanny expectation, desert sands, starry skies, passing clouds.

The fourth group, under the heading of jazz is, I feel, a much neglected field. There are a great number of pieces here – sad, vital, evocative – and all with definite and appealing rhythm, which are very useful in assembly presentations with children. I have found instrumental blues recordings most useful – Chris Barber's 'Chimes Blues', Louis

Armstrong's 'Tin Roof Blues'. With such pieces being played in the background, readings of poems like Auden's 'Funeral Blues' and Vachel Lindsay's 'That Daniel Jazz' take on an added dimension.

Assemblies are much more satisfactory if the hymns are enjoyable to sing, have words that make some sense to children and a simple accompaniment. As no one hymn anthology would seem to meet everybody's needs it is often a good policy to choose the one that is most suited for the specific needs of the school and buy this in bulk. A few individual copies of other hymn books could then be obtained, and specially chosen items could be taken from these as and when is thought necessary.

To suit the needs of the average primary school it would be hard to better the BBC hymn book, *Come and Praise*. There is a book of accompaniments, most of which would be well within the range of a moderate pianist, children's copies are in a clear and simple format, and there is also a record with excellent sung versions of twenty-one of the hymns and songs in the book. This hymn anthology contains seventy-two pieces and these are an excellent mixture of traditional and original – 'He's got the whole world in His Hands'; 'Join with us to sing God's praises'; 'Travel on'; 'Autumn days'; 'Think of a world without any flowers'; 'Praise Him'.

For Infants and the bottom end of the junior school, the Galliard Book, *Hello World*, is most useful. The songs in this book are linked with themes such as: Experience, Language, Bible . . . and young children really do enjoy both the words and music.

A. and C. Black's *Someone's Singing Lord* is a very popular anthology which offers much that appeals to the middle of the junior school. Again there is considerable originality ('Milk bottle tops and paper bags') and lively accompaniments, many of which are scored for percussion, recorders, chime bars etc. The Galliard *Faith, Folk* series of hymn books are always valuable, and *New Orbit* from the same publisher is the sort of hymn book no junior school should be without. This contains a really thoughtful selection of hymns (many of which are recommended in the Class Assemblies section of this book), which are enough to cover the needs of the whole school year.

This brings us to a consideration of children accompanying the singing in assembly and providing musical offerings of their own. Schools vary enormously in terms of teachers' musical talents, instruments available, room to perform adequately etc., but some form of children's musical participation in assembly is very worthwhile.

To build up a repertoire of musical arrangements for children to play in assembly takes time, and those who are just beginning the exercise may find it advantageous to start with basics. The first accompaniment of singing could be by clapping hands. A book that recognises this is *Someone's Singing Lord* and *ostinato* is introduced as early as the second hymn in this useful collection.

Once this awareness of rhythm, clapping and the 'beat' of hymns and songs has been recognised, the building-up of a percussion section for school use could follow naturally. Instruments that might be acquired could include a drum (10 in Everplay); a glockenspiel (Granton 21 note, chromatic C4); xylophones (alto – New Era 9666, bass – New Era 9663). More mundane items such as tambours, chime bars, coconut shells, claves could also be used and, if finances will run to it, a beautiful sound can be had from a base metallaphone (Studio 49 Bmd).

To 'front' this grouping of instruments there could be a recorder section, perhaps composed of descants, tenors and trebles.

Books like *Someone's Singing Lord* and *Come and Praise* offer many opportunities for an instrumental group, built up around the instruments described, to accompany the singing of hymns. Assemblies are improved even further if the instrumentalists regularly play something in their own right. This could be entry or departure music, or a piece that has a place of its own during an assembly. For some useful material here see the resources section that follows.

Sources

Useful records

'Come and Praise', 21 songs for assembly, by the Coloma Convent Grammar School, BBC REC 317 Stereo.

'Negro Spirituals Anthology', The Golden Gate Quartet, Columbia 2C 062 11993

'More Folk in Worship', The Crown Folk, BBC REC 176 Stereo.

'The World of Songs for Sunday', Nigel Brooks Singers, Decca SPA 482.

'Folk in Worship', The Crown Folk, BBC REC 58M.

Respighi, Rimsky-Korsakov and Mussorgsky, Helidor 2548 267.

'Favourite Marches', Tchaikovsky, Strauss, Verdi, Berlioz, Wills CFP 40254.

'These You have Loved', EMI CFP 40277.

'The World of Great Classics – Overtures' ('William Tell', 'Midsummer Night's Dream' etc.) Decca SPA 92

'Ambassador Satch', Louis Armstrong, Phillips BBL 7091.

'Out of this World', BBC Radiophonic Workshop, BBC REC 225 Stereo.

'Sound Effects No. 6', BBC RED 106M.

All these records contain material I have used often. It covers the fields of Classical, Folk/Religious, Sound Effects and Jazz, as described in the text.

Readers would, of course, find other selections equally suitable and availability is obviously a most important factor here.

Useful hymn books

Come and Praise, pub. BBC
Hello World, pub. Galliard
Someone's Singing Lord, pub. A. and C. Black
Faith, Folk and . . . Festivity/Nativity/Clarity, pub. Galliard
New Orbit, pub. Galliard
Something to Sing, Something to Sing Again and *Something to Sing at Assembly*, all by G. Brace, pub. CUP.

These hymn books contain many simple arrangements that can be used for percussion and recorder groups. When the latter are to perform without singers, the next section will prove helpful.

Useful material for instrumental pieces

6 into 37, by Graham Whettam, pub. Leeds Music Co. – a combination of thirty-seven pieces from six ideas for descant/tenor/treble recorders.
Hickety Pickety, percussion arrangements by Avril Dankworth (also includes songs by Mervyn Butch), pub. Chappell and Co.
Fly Roun', by Anne Mendoza, pub. OUP.
10 European Folk Songs, arranged by A.W. Benoy, pub. Novello. This is a delightful collection which offers that unbeatable combination of being easy to play yet sounding quite sophisticated and accomplished.
For something longer that can be used to show off the talents of the really good players, selections from the following could be used:
Oh Noah, by Clive Sansom, pub. Studio Music.
Captain Noah and his Floating Zoo, pub. Novello.
Holy Moses, pub. Novello.

A further source of specially tailored, and attractive arrangements for recorder and percussion groups is Panda Music, 79 Pinewood Avenue, Crowthorne, Berks. RG11 6RR.

H1 Gifts

Medium Rock Tempo — Words and Music by Olive Kershaw

Blue, blue, blue is the sky — Green, green, green is the grass — tall, tall, tall is the tree — giv-en to you and giv-en to me —

1. God made the world He worked to a plan — in it cre-a-ted a woman and man, — "Now" He said, "the

Chorus
Gifts, Gifts, Gifts from above,
Gifts, Gifts, Gifts with His love
Gifts, Gifts, all of them free,
Given to you, and given to me.

2. Man multiplied all over the earth
Treasures from God, had found a new worth,
Greedy, Selfish, Man wanted more
And with this aim, he started a war.

Chorus

3. God sent His son, to show us the way.
Ignorant man said, 'Now He shall pay'.
The supreme gift, he nailed to the cross.
How little man knew, how great his loss.

Chorus

4. God was angered, and saddened by man,
He would not fit in with His divine plan.
Greedy man has created hell.
If there is hope, then, just time will tell.

Chorus

98 *Music and Assembly*

H2 All the nations

Words by Michael Cockett

Music by Kevin Mayhew

With life

mf

G   C   Am   D   G

Chorus

All the na-tions of the earth praise the Lord who

G   C   Am

brings to brith the great-est star, the smallest flower.

D   G   C

Fine *Verse*

Al - le - lu - ia.   1. Let the hea - vens

Am   D   G

2 Snow-capped mountains, praise the Lord
Alleluia;
Rolling hills, praise the Lord
Alleluia.

Chorus

3 Deep sea water, praise the Lord
Alleluia;
Gentle rain, praise the Lord
Alleluia.

Chorus

4 Roaring lion, praise the Lord
Alleluia;
Singing birds, praise the Lord
Alleluia.

Chorus

5 Kings and princes, praise the Lord,
Alleluia;
Young and old, praise the Lord
Alleluia.

H3 The family of love

Geoffrey Hericks

Moderato

1. Join in the song of the family of love, Praise God who sent us his son from above Father and Friend to his people in need; : Lord of our lives and our Saviour indeed.

2 God is the giver of all that we use;
   Giving and sharing we cannot refuse.
   Brothers and sisters with all of mankind,
   Leaving our sorrows and hardships behind.

   Chorus

3 God is our Father whose love never ends,
   Binding together our families and friends;
   Ending our warfare and bringing us peace,
   Born to a family whose love will not cease.

   Chorus

4 Gladness and joy fill our hearts as we sing
   Songs of thanksgiving to Jesus our King.
   Glorious moments and long-treasured days,
   Love that he shows us in so many ways.

   Chorus

H4 The Lord's my shepherd

Cecily Taylor

Smoothly and flowing

1. The Lord's my Shep-herd I am sure of all his love, I need no more: Con-tent in pas-tures I will lie For all my needs he'll sa-tis-fy.

2 Beside the waters of his peace
  My aching heart can find release,
  And for his very own name's sake
  He guides and shows the path to take.

3 No valley's shadow dark as death
  Need cause me fear nor quivering breath,
  For in the darkness he will be
  With crook and staff to comfort me.

4 My foes will see the feast he spreads,
  Like oil his blessings bathe my head;
  With joy my life will overflow
  Wherever I may chance to go.

5 The love and goodness of his ways
  Will follow me for all my days,
  And I shall dwell where I belong –
  Within his house my whole life long.

H5 Shelter the weak

Words by Peter Westmore

Music by Edward Hughes

Brightly

Chorus

Shel-ter the weak;— give to the poor— If you seek heav-en, here is the door.— Shel-ter the weak— and you will see,— when you do this,— you shel-ter Me— when you do this,— you shel-ter Me———

Verse
I came to save the human race; I chose a humble resting place. There were but few enlightened men who welcomed Me in Bethlehem
All those of you who tend the poor Bring presents to My stable door. With open arms I greet all men Who welcome Me in Bethehlehem.
F B F C7 F B♭ F C7 F B♭ F B♭ F B♭ F
1.
2. D.S. al Coda
Coda
ritard.
Shelter me
C7 B♭ F

Prayers and 'Thoughts'

The traditional assembly suited actions to words and it was usual to close the eyes and put the hands together to pray. Many people still feel that linking words and actions in this way is an essential part of any service. Others, however, feel that these customs are not necessarily important.

Clearly, in schools both attitudes are reflected in assemblies. More important than taking a hard and fast line on either of these issues perhaps, is looking at what creates the right 'atmosphere' in an assembly. The reality of being part of a caring community is obviously essential and the approach to any prayers could be based on how this is achieved. The words of Gladys Bennett and John Tearnan, writing in *Hello World* seem particularly appropriate here: 'The whole intention and purpose of coming together as a community creates the possibility of worship, and is in itself the beginning of worship.'

This section of the book, therefore, offers suggestions to teachers of material for that period in assembly set aside for quiet reflection. Some prayers are included, as are some 'thoughts'. There is also a list of themes appropriate to both.

P1 Joy

In this morning hour
I want a fresh chance
To start again.
I don't want to waste the minutes and hours
That have been given to me.
I want to be alive
To every experience,
In conversation,
In the mundane tasks of this day.
In moments of relaxation
I want to find joy in living.
Lord of the morning, help me.

Extract from a poem by Frank Topping

P2 Optimism

Woman in the bus with a pram and a baby
and a shopping bag crammed that jammed right in her way:
Clippy helped her off with the pram and the baby
and one sun shone in my own dark day.

Blind man in the street with no four-footed rover
But a painted white stick that tapped along the way:
Young man took his arm and with care crossed him over,
and two suns shone in my own dark day.

Server in the shop with poor head a-spinning,
and the aching feet she must bear to earn her pay:
Served me with a smile and a manner most winning
and three suns shone in my own dark day.

Landed back at home when my errands were ended,
But the people I'd met just wouldn't go away:
Found my broken heart had been marvellously mended,
and darkness driven from my sunny day.

Sister Oswin

P3 Disappointment

Let us think this morning about disappointments. Sometimes we say to ourselves: 'If only I'd done that . . . if only I'd been there then . . . if only I could have . . .'

Often, however, if we look back, something that disappointed us at the time led on to other happenings in our lives.

Let us try to learn from these disappointments so that we do not think 'if only'. Let us think instead that because one thing happened another took place.

P4 Being useful

O Lord
Let us not live to be useless;
For Christ's sake.   Amen.

John Wesley

P5 Being prepared

May our eyes see the need for things to be done,
Our ears be prepared to listen to cries for help,
Our mouths used to give encouragement and not insults,
Our hands be useful,
Our minds ready to consider suggestions and change.

P6 Time

Lord help us to remember that every day is a gift. May we not take it for granted but use it as wisely and as well as possible. Help us always to have time for the right kind of work and action.

P7 Encouragement

Prayer found in Chester Cathedral.

Give me a good digestion, Lord
And always something to digest;
Give me a healthy body, Lord,
With sense to keep it at its best.

Give me a healthy mind, good Lord,
To keep the good and pure in sight,
Which seeing sin is not appalled
But finds a way to set it right.

Give me a mind that is not bored,
That does not whimper, whine or sigh;
Don't let me worry overmuch
About the fussy thing called I.

Give me a sense of humour, Lord,
Give me the grace to see a joke,
To get some happiness from life
And pass it on to other folk.

Anon.

P8 Home

Let us think about the homes we have left this morning. Let us think about those who are away from their homes or who find life at home difficult and troublesome.

Let us think about the homes we return to after school. Let us value the things we find in our homes which make us feel cared for and loved.

P9 Modern blessings

In our prayers this morning let us be grateful for the fact that we live today, and not in some of the more difficult times of the past. Let us be grateful for the fact that our towns and villages provide houses and flats in which we can live so much more comfortably than children did years ago.

Let us remember that in Preston in 1845 a government health investigation found that in 442 houses there were only 852 beds, but 2,400 people slept in them.

Let us be grateful for the comfort and good health we are mostly able to enjoy today.

P10 Wisdom

He who knows himself is enlightened
He who conquers himself is mighty

Tao saying

P11 Nature

At man's harnessing of the powers of nature,
of flood and tide,
of coal and oil,
of atomic power,
of nuclear fission . . .
We wonder and stand in silent admiration.

J. and E. Young

P12 Inspiring people

Let us think this morning about people whose lives inspire us by their example. We might think of people whose courage we can read about and see on our television screens. We might think of saints who often gave their lives for what they believed. We might think of people we know who never complain even though they may be ill or in pain.

Let us think about learning from the qualities of others and hope that in our own lives we can show courage, kindness, patience and understanding.

P13 Examining ourselves

Have I let brambles grow where once there was wheat?
Have I been insensible to poor men's needs?
Have I put all my trust in gold?
Have I gloated over my great wealth?
Have I taken pleasure in my enemy's misfortune?

From the Book of Job

P14 Love

Love is something we all want to give and receive.
Love is easy to give to someone we know and like.
Love is difficult to give to someone who is irritating and has unpleasant habits.
Love is difficult to give when it means giving up time and effort for people who don't seem to care.
But:
If you only love those who love you what credit is that to you?

Adapted from St Matthew

P15 Are you a good person to know?

Let us have real warm affection for one another as between brothers, and a willingness to let the other man have the credit.
Share the happiness of those who are happy and the sorrow of those who are sad.
Don't become snobbish but take a real interest in ordinary people.
Don't pay back a bad turn by a bad turn.
Don't become set in your own opinions.

From a letter from St Paul to Christians in Rome

P16 Those in need

Let us think this morning of the many people in our country who need help. These might include:
those who are sick,
those who have been injured in accidents, and their families,
those who are handicapped in some way and can't live without help,
women with small children and no husband,
those whose houses are not fit for them to live in,
those who find it difficult to get a job,
those who have 'dropped out' and have no homes or job,
those who suffer from mental illness,
those who are too old to look after themselves.

P17 Advice

Be free from:
hate
arrogance
selfishness
changes of mood
impatience
discontent
unreliability
unfaithfulness
temptation
intolerance

From the Hindu poem: 'The Gita'

P18 Rules to think about

Don't:
refuse to help the poor
be cruel to the needy
deny the hungry
be mean to those who need money
avoid people you think poorer than you.

Do:
respect people in authority
speak to everybody politely
help widows and orphans
give as generously as you can
share people's sorrows
visit the sick.

Adapted from Ecclesiasticus 4

P19 Living together (1)

Oh God
Let us be united
Let us speak in harmony.

Hindu prayer

P20 Living together (2)

Share each other's troubles and problems.

Galations 6:2

P21 Ourselves (1)

Be worthy of a reputation

Confucius

P22 Ourselves (2)

All that we are is the result of our thoughts.

Buddha

P23 Eternal truths

The world is preserved by three things:
truth
justice
peace

Jewish saying

P24 Unselfishness

He is best loved who does most good to other creatures.

Islamic saying

P25 A recommendation

Earn all you can
Save all you can
Give all you can.

John Wesley

P26 Planning for the future

Give a man a fish and you feed him for a day,
Teach a man to fish and you feed him for life.

Confucius

P27 Guidance

Wisdom leads to peace.

Hindu saying

P28 Forgiveness

Forgive me for
Losing my temper when I should have controlled it;
Allowing my tongue to run away with me when I should have kept quiet;
Allowing myself to have bitter feelings about someone else;
Refusing to listen to good advice and for resenting correction when I deserved it.
Forgive me for
Failing to do things as well as I could have done them,
Failing to finish the tasks I should have finished;
Failing to work my hardest at my lessons and my work, and to play my hardest at my games.
Forgive me for everything that I meant to do and failed to do, and for everything that I meant not to do and did.
This I ask for Jesus' sake.

Part of a prayer by William Barclay

P29 The world at large

Let us think about what we can learn from people in other parts of the world. There are many who think that at some time in every day we should stop what we are doing and think about the importance of our families and friends.

Let us never be too busy to think of others.

P30 Admiration

When we think of
  the courage which takes men to the stars,
  the spirit of adventure in the voyage of the space ship,
  the scientific accuracy of the satellite's orbit,
  the thrust of the rocket
    into silence,
    beyond the pull of earth . . .
We wonder, and stand in silent admiration.

Part of 'An Act of Wonder', by J. and E. Young

P31 Being content

Let us think about contentment. The following words were written by St Paul in a letter to the Christians at Philippi, about the year AD 62.

'Fix your minds on what is true and just . . . I know how to live when things are difficult and when things are prosperous. I have everything I want – in fact I am rich. Yes I am quite content.'

The amazing thing about these words is that they were written by St Paul when he was in prison.

Let us learn to try and find contentment even when our lives seem very difficult.

P32 Being generous

Let us learn to:
Give and not count the cost,
Work and not look for rest
Or always think about what is the reward.

Adapted from St Ignatius

P33 A special journey

Let us think about our own 'journeys through life'. Let us think about when we travel fastest; when we ought to have most wisdom; when we might be most in need of help.

By thinking about these things we may be more understanding of people of all ages at all times.

P34 Life savers

Let us think about those people who spend their lives saving the lives of others. Sometimes this is done in very dangerous circumstances. Let us think particularly about the Royal National Lifeboat Institution.

Since its foundation in 1824 those who man its lifeboats have saved the lives of over 100,000 people.

P35 Fame

Let us now sing the praises of famous men, the heroes of our nation's history. *Ecclesiasticus 44.*
These words help us to remember those famous people who, by their courage or kindness or wisdom, inspire our own lives.

P36 A protest

We protest
about people who are careless about looking
after our towns and villages,
about laziness in helping others, about greed and
selfishness, about dishonesty and vandalism.

P37 Using time well

Let us think about, and value, time. The following words, which were written by a nine year old girl, might help us to do this.

>Time is coming
>Time is going
>Time is here
>Time has gone.

P38 Learning from others

Let us try to build a better world by learning from books. In 1902 a man called Jack London wrote a book about the terrible conditions that he found in London. This book is called *The People of the Abyss.*

In it Jack London describes how he dressed as a 'typical' unemployed man so that people would not notice him. Dressed in a ragged suit and dirty cloth-cap he slept and ate in a workhouse and wandered the streets at night. He saw men so hungry that they searched the gutters for orange peel to eat. Most of all he felt sorry for the thin, starving, ragged children.

P39 Giving sensibly

There is an old Japanese saying: 'The beggar was given a horse.' He did not want a horse, only a meal.
   Let us think when we give or help others so that we contribute what is most useful.

P40 Everybody

For the healing of the nations,
Lord, we pray with one accord;
For a just and equal sharing
of the things that earth affords.
To a life of love in action
help us rise and pledge our word.

Fred Kaan

P41 Hate

Hatred is like rain in the desert
It is of no use to anybody

African proverb

P42 Think before you speak

A word is like water
Once spilled it cannot be gathered again.

African proverb

P43 Something learned

Let us learn from
the past
our mistakes
each other.

P44 God guides

God, our Father, you can make all things new.
We commit ourselves to you: help us
to live for others since your love includes all men,
to seek those truths which we have not yet seen,
to obey your commands which we have heard but not yet obeyed,
to trust each other in the fellowship you have given us,
and may we be renewed, by your Spirit, through Jesus Christ, your son and our Lord.

An Uppsala prayer from the 1968 World Council of Churches

P45 Honesty

Let us think about:
being honest and admitting when we are wrong;
being honest about our own faults;
being honest when it is easier to tell a lie;
being honest in our opinions even if they don't always make us popular.

P46 What is important?

If you talk to gold it will not answer you.
If you talk to cloth it will not answer you. What really counts is man.

Ghanian proverb

P47 Enjoyment

Let us be thankful for:
those people who entertain us and make us laugh;
those who write books or music we enjoy;
sports stars who thrill us with their achievements;
those who make things we enjoy using and playing with;
those people who are always cheerful and a pleasure to be with.

P48 Modesty

When you help people, don't 'blow your trumpet' like people who are only pretending to be good; they want people to say, 'He's a good fellow!' Very good. They get what they want.

When you help people, don't let your right hand know what your left hand is doing; help people without others noticing it.

Matthew 6:2-3; *New World* version

Themes

With primary school children a word associated with a theme is a useful starting point for thoughts and prayers. The following is a list of themes well suited to this age group.

Advice	Easter	Language
Aims	Education	Light
Animals		Little things
	Family	Living together
Barriers	Favourites	Loneliness
Beauty	Fear	Love
Beginnings	Fire	
Birds	Food	Machines
	Foolishness	Mystery
Caring	Freedom	
Change	Friendship	Names
Christmas		Neighbours
Colour	Generosity	
Communications	Growth	Old age
Communities		Ourselves
Conversation	Handicaps	Overcoming difficulties
Courage	Hands	
Creation	Happiness	Patience
Customs	Healing	Peace
	Heroes	People who help us
Danger	Holidays	Pollution
Determination	Humour	Proverbs
Disappointment		
Disaster	Imagination	Qualities
Discovery	Injustice	
Duty		Race
	Journeys	Religion
	Joy	Remembering
		Rules

Safety	Strength	Violence
School	Superstition	War
Seasons	Talents	Waste
Senses	Time	Water
Signs and Symbols	Thanks	Wisdom
Shape		Words
Sharing	Usefulness	Work

Biblical Material

Reading passages from the Bible was once a more common practice in assemblies for young children than it is today. Such passages were often used without much thought as to relevance and comprehensibility.

The publication of Ronald Goldman's *Religious Thinking from Childhood to Adolescence* (pub. Routledge, Kegan and Paul in 1964) disturbed a great number of people by its suggestion that much of the teaching that had been Bible-based was ineffective.

The result of this was that many teachers in primary and lower secondary schools now felt reluctant to use Biblical material.

These two extremes of thought and practice seem to have become modified, if today's assemblies are the yardstick for judgement. Biblical material has its place as long as it is used thoughtfully, is kept short, and is taken from translations which aid comprehension for young children.

The creation (Genesis) is a very difficult concept, despite some dynamic poems about it. Perhaps the best way to approach it as assembly material is to consider what Christians believe the writers of Genesis meant by their words and stories.

Without being sidetracked into historical reality, a judicious choice of text (e.g. 1:29) could show that one of man's purposes on earth was to care for it. This could be developed to mention that early Biblical writers believed that man was alive 'to conquer the earth'. By this they meant, to enjoy it, find out its secrets, and use this knowledge to provide a better way of life. Man has done a great deal of 'conquering'.

> At man's harnessing of the powers of nature,
> of flood and tide,
> of coal and oil,
> of atomic power,
> of nuclear fission . . .
> We wonder and stand in silent admiration.

From a prayer by J. and E. Young

There is still a great deal he does not know however:
> We are a small part of the earth;
> The earth is a planet in the solar system;
> The solar system is part of a galaxy;
> There are other galaxies in the universe;
> The universe is getting bigger.

It is tempting to use parables in primary school assemblies, but like many things in the Bible they often have complex meanings. Perhaps it would be fair to say that parables offer something for reflection, rather than firm indications of how we should behave. With young children it seems best to prepare the background of the parable, tell it simply, and refrain from further moralising.

As a source for parables, beautifully told, Alan Dale's *New World – the heart of the New Testament in Plain English* (pub. OUP), would be hard to beat. As with all Biblical material, time spent 'setting the scene' and presenting background material is always time well spent.

Young children in today's society have little idea of the background against which Bible stories and events are set. This applies not merely to geography, climate and clothing but also to things like structures.

For instance, the following points could be examined and explained in more detail: the Jewish father at the time of Jesus was the virtual ruler of his household, with wife and daughters dedicated to looking after men and home; religion was a part of the daily life in the home – not just a weeky gathering in a communal building; the church (synagogue) was a place of learning; fathers usually passed on their trade to their sons.

Other points, useful for background knowledge of Biblical events might include: the difficulty and slowness of journeys; the need for regular 'camps' when making journeys of only modest distances by today's standards; nomadic and town life; the cramped nature of walled towns; the smallness, by our standards, of the villages outside the towns; the great disparity between rich and poor, healthy and unhealthy.

Again, for the teacher who wishes to have useful material on hand to help build up this background picture, there are some excellent books available. Recommended are: *Everyday Life in Old Testament Times*, by E.W. Heaton, pub. Carousel; the 'Getting to Know About . . .' in the *Lands of the Bible* series, edited by Diana Prickett, pub. Denholm House Press.

Much useful work can be done by a closer examination of the Bible itself. Since the Bible is a collection of books compiled over a long period of time, we would inevitably expect some discrepancies. The content of the Bible in terms of laws, poetry, history, letters, gospels and symbolic stories could be looked at. Examples that might be used as illustrations here: Deuteronomy, as indicating laws which the Hebrew people had to follow (5:16–20); a psalm as an example of poetry; the beginning of 1 Kings 6 as history; letters from St Paul; gospels relating to the Christmas story; symbolic stories as epitomised in Luke 20:8–18. Another point that might be made is that much of what was written in the Bible was done long after the events described had taken place.

Children are often interested to know that the Bible was originally written on papyrus. The Greek word for papyrus is 'byblos' – hence 'Bible'. The original language used in its Old Testament compilation was Hebrew. This is written from right to left and has no vowels in the written words. See illustration for example of Hebrew script.

שְׁמַע יִשְׂרָאֵל יְהוָה אֱלֹהֵינוּ יְהוָה אֶחָד

Hear, O Israel: the Lord our God, the Lord is one

This is taken from 'Getting to know about Learning and Playing' in the *Lands of the Bible* series.

There were early translations of the Bible into English by Bede in 735, and Tyndale, in his English New Testament of 1526. The world's most expensive book is the hand-written copy of the Bible called the Codex Sinaiticus. It is sixteen hundred years old and was bought from Russia, after the revolution, by the British government. The price paid was £100,000. It is kept in the British Museum. The Bible is also the world's best selling book.

The references that follow are intended to help the teacher with a Bible source that could be consulted in connection with a wide variety of themes that often occur in primary schools.

Theme	Source
Awe	Psalm 29.
Barriers	Luke 7: 1–10; Luke 19: 1–9; Luke 15: 11–32.
Beginnings	Joshua 1: 6–8; Ruth 1: 14–18.
Bread	John 6: 5–13.
Building	Chronicles Books 1 and 2.
Celebration	Judges 9: 26–7.
Courage	1 Samuel 17: 20–37, 40–53.
Determination	Matthew 15.
Distress	2 Samuel 13: 15–22.
Exploration	Exodus 13: 17–22.
Eyes	Matthew 5: 29; Mark 3: 5; Luke 22: 61.
Faith	Daniel 6: 1–28; Mark 2: 1–12; James 2: 14–17.
Family	1 Corinthians 12: 13–27; John 19: 26–7.
Foolishness	Luke 12: 13–21; Proverbs 3: 13–20.
Forgiveness	Luke 15: 11–32; Luke 23: 32–4; Colossians 3: 12–17.
Freedom	Exodus 21: 1–6.
Friendship	1 Samuel 19: 1–10.
Generosity/Concern	Mark 6: 30–44; Luke 21: 1–4.
Hands	Mark 3: 1–6; Matthew 27: 24–6; Genesis 14: 22–4; 2 Kings 10: 15.
Harvest	Matthew 13: 1–9; Matthew 13: 24–30; Matthew 20: 1–16.
Journeys	Matthew 2: 13–33.
Laughter	Ecclesiastes 3: 4.
Lost	Luke 15: 3–7.
Love	1 Corinthians 13: 1–13; John 19: 26–7.
Loyalty	Genesis 37: 12–24.
Money	Luke 18: 18–33.
Names	Matthew 16: 16–18.
News	Mark 1: 16–34.
Obedience	Luke 2: 41–52.
Overcoming difficulties	Luke 10: 25–37.
Peace	Romans 12: 9–18; Matthew 5: 9.
Prayer	1 Kings 8: 22–32.
Priorities	Luke 10: 25–37.
Shame	Matthew 26: 75.
Sickness	Luke 17: 11–19; Mark 7: 31–35.
Song	Psalm 23.
Spirit of Service	Mark 14: 32–42.
Symbol of affection and treachery	Acts 20: 36–8. Matthew 26: 47–50.
Sympathy	Luke 7: 1–10.
Time	Ecclesiastes 3: 1–15.

Unselfishness	Romans 12: 1–5; Ecclesiastes 4: 1–11.
Warnings	1 Samuel 26: 2–12.
Water	Mark 1: 4–9.
Wisdom	1 Kings 3: 4–15; Job 28: 12–20.
Words	James 3: 1–10.
Work	Matthew 25: 14–19; Matthew 25: 31–45; Ecclesiasticus 38: 27–34.

Assemblies and Religions

There are many schools where children of non-European cultures and religions are present in large numbers. This is bound to be a significant factor in the planning of assemblies. Other schools, even with a majority of pupils of European culture, may feel that multi-religious considerations should be a feature of their assemblies.

In this section, therefore, an attempt has been made to give teachers a simple outline of non-Christian religions. A detailed list of helpful books is appended.

Once again, the need to present children with information in language that is comprehensible to them is vitally important. The information given in this section would therefore need to be adapted to specific children's needs and abilities. Difficult words mentioned could well be supported by always writing them where the children can see them.

Religion in a multi-racial society

With primary school children in mind, it is obviously most fruitful to concentrate on religions that are substantially represented in Britain. Thus whilst Taoism and Shintoism have more adherents worldwide than Judaism, it is the latter that is more significant here.

It may also be worthwhile for teachers to think about a comment by the Rev. A.E. Perry in his book *How People Worship* (pub. Denholm House Press and E.J. Arnold):

'Two way traffic applies . . . in the worship of a God – whatever one's religion. On one side there is the worth – the nature, or character – of the God, and on the other the response men make to him, in word and action. Depending on the character of the God, the response may be one of awe and wonder, or fear, or penitence, or joy, or love, or a combination of a number of these things. But whatever it is, the two basic aspects of worship are always there: the God's character, and man's response.'

Islam

(a) *Belief*

Islam is the name of the Muslim religion and the word Islam means 'submission to the will of God'. Mohammed was the founder of the religion and he was a descendant of the Biblical patriarch Abraham. Mohammed was born on 20th April, 571. Islamic belief is summed up in the Muezzin's call (below).

(b) *Place of worship*

The place of worship for a Muslim is a mosque. Mosques are often richly ornamented with mosaics. Inside the mosque there is a niche in the wall, which is called the Mihrab. This is placed so that when the congregation face it they are also facing Mecca.

(c) *Prayer*

Muslims are called to prayer five times a day by the Muezzin, who makes his call from a minaret on the mosque. Translated, his call is: 'God is most great. I testify that Mohammed is God's apostle. I testify there is no God but Allah. Come to prayer. Come to security. God is most great.'

Rarely can a Muslim attend a mosque for all his prayers (at daybreak, midday, mid-afternoon, after sunset, at night). He therefore prostrates himself on a prayer mat so that not only can he be clean when he prays, but he can also make sure that the area of his praying is clean.

When a Muslim prays, he first of all stands with his hands raised to his ears, then with his arms folded across his chest, then lying on the floor. Whilst he is in these positions he recites prayers and passages from the Koran.

(d) Sacred writings

The sacred book of the Muslims is the Koran. This contains the words that were brought to Mohammed by the angel Gabriel. The first thing a Muslim learns from the Koran is the Kalimah – 'There is only one God and Mohammed is the last of the prophets.'

The Koran is written in Arabic.

(e) Religious practice

A Muslim must perform five acts of faith. These are called the 'Pillars of Islam'. They are:
1 Belief in God.
2 Salat – praying five times a day.
3 Zakat – the giving of 1/40th of one's income to the poor.
4 Ramadan – a month of fasting when nothing is eaten between sunrise and sunset.
5 Hajj – a pilgrimage to the Holy City of Mecca (in Saudi-Arabia), which all Muslims hope to make at least once in their lives.

(f) Festive occasions

1 Celebration of Mohammed's birthday.
2 Id-ul-Fitr (the 'little feast'), which celebrates the end of Ramadan. Present-giving takes place at this festival.
3 Id-ul-Adha is the festival held at the end of a pilgrimage to Mecca. For four days devotees pray, offer meat sacrifices and give to the poor.

Useful books related to Islam

Nahda's Family, by M. Blakeley, pub. A. and C. Black.
This is written in documentary style with photographs. It is about a Muslim girl living in the North of England.
Mohhamed, by Bernard Brett, pub. Collins.
A book best used by teacher and top juniors together. It has an objective approach and is written by a non-Muslim.
The Arab World, by Shirley Kay, pub. OUP.
Useful for tracing the beginnings of Islam.
The Way of the Muslim, by Dr M. Iqbal, pub. Hulton.
This is a very useful book from 'The Way of. . .' series. The author is a Muslim and a teacher and has participated in Schools' Council projects on RE. The book can be used with 9–13 year olds.

Miscellaneous material related to Islam

Music – in recent years the Horniman museum has had an exhibition of musical instruments from the Middle East. A useful publication stemmed from this: *Music and Musical Instruments in the World of Islam* (pub. Horniman Museum, London Road, Forest Hill, London SE23).

For pictures of Middle East countries, the most topical are in brochures etc., provided by the Tourist Offices of the various countries.

A set of slides on 'Islamic calligraphy and illuminations' can be obtained from the British Museum.

Hinduism

(a) Belief

Hinduism is not a religion in the same sense as Islam. It is the name given to religion in India. This has many strands and there is no single set of beliefs. Many Hindus in Britain are theists and believe that there is one supreme God, referred to as Brahman, who is represented in many different ways through Gods and Goddesses – Vishnu, Krishna, Rama, Shiva, Ganesha, etc. Hindus believe that everyone is reborn many thousands of times and that the way a person lives in this life will determine what kind of life he will have next time.

(b) Festive occasions

In the north of India holy days of Hinduism are many and complex, but the best known of the great festivals are as follows:

1 Dassera ('ten special days'), in September/October, celebrates one of Rama's victories over Ravana.
2 Diwali, or Dipawali, is the spectacular Festival of Lights, in October/November, which symbolises the triumph of good over evil, light over darkness. Lights are placed in temples, houses and streets; music and dancing take place everywhere; special dishes are eaten and presents are exchanged.
3 Shivarati is a night of worship dedicated to Shiva, near the end of winter.
4 Holi is the great Spring Festival. People throw coloured powders and coloured water. To be covered with both is a sign that the day has been well celebrated.

Useful books related to Hinduism

The Way of the Hindu, by Swami Yogeshananda, pub. Hulton. Another useful book from this series on religions.
India and her neighbours, by Taya Zinkin, pub. OUP. An excellent book on ancient and modern India which includes much on beliefs and customs.
Indian Tales and Legends, by J.E.B. Gray, pub. OUP. Contains amongst the stories some from both the Mahabharata and the Ramayana.
A Hindu Family in Britain, by Peter Bridger, pub. Religious Education Press. Useful background material for upper juniors.
Understanding your Hindu Neighbour, by John Ewan, pub. Lutterworth. The preceding books are all useful for facts. Those which follow are fiction.
The faithful parrot and other Indian folk stories, by Taya Zinkin, pub. OUP. An attractive book, which deals with much of the Hindu mythology; best suited to top juniors.
The moody peacock and other Indian folk tales, pub. Studio Vista. Simple stories and good illustrations.
Indian Village Tales, by Prafulla Mohanti, pub. Davis-Poynter. Some marvellous tales, many well suited to assembly, but often told with a crudity that many teachers will eliminate before re-telling to children.
One man and his dog, by Henry Lefever, pub. Lutterworth. A mixture of Hindu and Buddhist tales. They are well told, good stories and, bearing in mind the complexity of some of the names (Dhritarashtra, Yuddisthira), there is a useful appendix on pronunciation.

Miscellaneous material related to Hinduism

Books from India (32 Coptic Street, London WC1) is a specialist book shop containing a good range of children's books. They also supply the latter to Foyles.
Music: records of Indian music, recorded in India, can be obtained from specialist Asian shops. Indian music on English labels is also available, e.g.: 'Music from India', HMV–EMI, an eight-record set featuring Ravi Shankar, Vilayat Khan etc.

Buddhism

(a) Belief

Buddhists believe that the cycle of birth, re-birth and suffering can only be ended by attaining 'Nirvana'. This means the 'blowing away' of all selfish desires and is achieved by following the Eightfold Path, in which a correct way is applied to concentration, mindfulness, endeavour, livelihoods, action, speech, resolve, viewpoint.

Buddhism originated with a wealthy Indian prince called Gautama, who lived from 563 to 483 BC. He was a Hindu and was so concerned with the poverty and suffering he saw round him that he believed peace could only be achieved by acceptance of the impermanence and suffering of life, deep meditation, and complete lack of self-interest. He became a monk and was known as 'the Buddha' – 'the Enlightened One'.

(b) Place of worship

Buddhists make gifts of candles and flowers before images of Buddha in temples. They also go to monasteries to offer gifts to the monks and to join them in religious chants.

(c) Meditation

Apart from their devotions in the temple, Buddhists pray before the family shrine in their own homes. A Thervada Buddhist might stand before the candle-lit shrine and say the Three Refuges:

> I go to the Buddha as my Refuge;
> I go to the Dhamma (Teaching) as my Refuge;
> I go to the Sangha (Monks) as my Refuge.

Special prayers are also said at every full and half moon.

(d) Religious practice

Buddhists seek to follow the Five Precepts, in which they promise not to kill, not to steal, not to indulge in sexual misconduct or falsehood, not to indulge in drugs or drink.

(e) Festive occasions

1 Wesak (Vesakha-Puja) is the great three-day feast of the Buddhist Full Moon Festival (early summer in our calendar). It combines the celebrations of the Buddha's birth, enlightenment and death. Food and gifts are distributed, houses decorated with flowers and lanterns and captive birds released.
2 Asalha-Puja (summer) is a celebration of the Buddha's first proclamation of the Truth – the Four Noble Truths and the Noble Eightfold Path.

Useful books related to Buddhism

The Festivals of Nepal, by Mary M. Anderson, pub. Allen and Unwin. A useful book for teachers' reference, with some excellent coloured photographs that could be used with the children.
Buddha, by Joan Lebold Cohen, pub. Macdonald.
The Life and Times of Buddha, by Gabriele Mandel Sugana, pub. Hamlyn.
The Buddha. Cambridge Introduction to the History of Mankind, by F.W. Rawding, pub. CUP.
The Way of the Buddha, by C.A. Burland, pub. Hulton.

The books just mentioned are mainly for information. For stories, the excellent *One Man and his Dog* is a good choice. For details of this see 'Useful books related to Hinduism'.

Miscellaneous material related to Buddhism

Collecting photographs of images of Buddha in various countries is interesting in that, whilst face and figure may differ according to local characteristics, the expression of tranquility and 'enlightenment' is apparent in all.

Judaism

(a) Belief

Orthodox Jews believe that there is one God, invisible and loving. The origins of the faith began with Abraham, 4,000 years ago, and with God's revelation to Moses on Sinai. Jews believe that God expects trust and dedication rather than fear and human sacrifice. Judaism is usually regarded as the faith from which both Christianity and Islam developed.

(b) Place of worship

The synagogue is where Jews meet to worship and study. Synagogues are plain buildings both inside and out. The congregation sit facing the direction of Jerusalem, and a curtain. Behind the curtain is a chest, known as the Ark of the Covenant. This chest is illuminated by a lamp that is never extinguished, and it contains the Torah (the scrolls of the Law).

The main time for worship is the Sabbath, which begins at sunset on a Friday and finishes about twenty-five hours later.

(c) Prayer

As soon as they get up in the morning Jews wash their hands and say a prayer of thanksgiving for the day. Prayers are said both before and after meals and special prayers mark the beginning of the Sabbath each week.

Prayers are important in both the synagogue and the home.

Men wear a skull cap and a prayer shawl (tallit) when praying in the synagogue, and each Jewish home has a small box on its doorstep. This is called a mezuzah and contains fifteen verses of Scripture. Jews entering the house touch the mezuzah to remind themselves that the home is a sacred place.

(d) Sacred writings

The Torah and the Talmud are the bases of Jewish sacred writing. The Torah is the first five books of the Bible – Genesis, Exodus, Leviticus, Numbers, Deuteronomy. Much discussion over many centuries centres on the Torah and, by about 500, this finally resulted in the Talmud being compiled. There are sixty-three books in the Talmud, which is not only an interpretation of the Torah but a Jewish encyclopedia of thought, experience and faith.

(e) Religious practice

The Jewish belief in God as the founder of everything is reinforced with reminders that Jews should never worship idols. Thus no likenesses of God appear anywhere (Second Commandment – 'Thou shalt not make thyself any graven image').

Jews also believe that as God is good so must his people be good. They try therefore to be conscious of duties to family and neighbours and to extend kindness and mercy to all.

(f) Festive occasions

1. The Jewish New Year is celebrated in October when trumpets (shofarim) of celebration are blown in the synagogue.
2. The tenth day of the Jewish New Year is Yom Kippur, the Day of Atonement. This is the most solemn day in the Jewish year, when members of the faith ask forgiveness for their sins.
3. Feast of Tabernacles (Sukkot). This joyful October feast reminds Jews of Moses leading them out of Egypt on the journey to Canaan.
4. Festival of Lights, or Hanukkah (December). When Judas Mac-

cabaeus defeated the Greeks in 165 BC, a great celebration was planned in the temple. The priests found, however, that there was not enough oil to keep the lamps burning until a new supply could be made. Nevertheless the lamps were lit and, by a miracle, burned for eight days.
5 Feast of Purim (March). This feast celebrates Esther and Mordecai's discovery of a plot to kill the Jews in 586 BC.
6 Feast of Passover (April). Prior to their escape from slavery in Egypt, Jewish homes were marked with blood on the doorpost so that God would 'pass over' them when killing the first-born of families in Egyptian homes. This feast and the great event of the Jews' escape from Egypt is celebrated by the eating of unleavened bread (bread made without yeast).
7 Feast of Pentecost, or Shavuot (May/June). Fifty days after the Feast of Passover the people praised God for giving them wheat for their bread.

Useful books related to Judaism

The Way of the Jew, by Rabbi Dr Louis Jacobs, pub. Hulton.
Understanding your Jewish Neighbour, by Myer Domnitz, pub. Lutterworth.
All about Jewish Holidays and Customs, by Morris Epstein, pub. Ktav (obtainable from 'Jerusalem the Golden', 146A Golders Green Road, London NW11).

The information books mentioned here are all suitable for use with children of upper primary school age. For stories there are:
The Magician, by Uli Shulevitz, pub. Collier Macmillan.
Zlateh the goat and other stories, by Isaac Bashevis Singer, pub. Longman.

Miscellaneous material related to Judaism

Music: 'Holiday and Festival Songs'. This record is on Tora Ben Tsvi AN 48-70 and is obtainable from 'Jerusalem the Golden', 146A Golders Green Road, London NW11.
Slide set: on Jewish Sabbath, available from The Slide Centre (Portmann House, 17 Broderick Road, London SW17 7DZ).
Film: 'Judaism', – FF289 is a film strip with notes and tape, available from Concordia Films (117 Golden Lane, London EC1).
  Useful addresses for further information about Judaism: Education Officer, Central Jewish Information Committee, Board of Deputies of British Jews, Woburn House, Upper Woburn Place, London WC1; or The Jewish National Fund, Harold Poster House, Kingsbury Circle, London NW9 9SP.

Further information regarding other religions

Five Religions in the Twentieth Century, by W. Owen Cole, pub. Hulton Educational, is a comprehensive look at religions today. A set of practical guidelines for use in selecting material can be obtained from: Centre for Urban Educational Studies, 34 Aberdeen Park, London N5 2BL.

Reminders

This section has several aims. First, it suggests a month by month sequence in which the stories and class assemblies detailed in this book might be used. Second, it provides reminders to teachers about stories of famous people, too well known at adult level to require further space spent on them here, but nevertheless valuable subjects to talk about with children.

Also included here are reminders of anniversaries and 'occasions'. Included with the last of these features are occasional Bible references and incidental pieces of information which can sometimes add an extra dimension when used in an assembly.

The basic main aim of the section is, therefore, to provide information that can be developed and extended as needed. This also applies to the list of 'inspiring lives' that is included at the end of the section and is grouped under related themes.

Stories and class assemblies

For ease of reference the school year rather than the calendar year is the arrangement used here. No story or assembly is used more than once but, again, it should be emphasised that the material is most adaptable and flexible.

September	S16, S19, S30, S36, S54, S69, S79, S81, A1, A2
October	S2, S10, S23, S26, S51, S64, S65, S77, A3, A4
November	S13, S30, S31, S37, S58, S62, S78, S80, A5, A6, A7
December	S1, S27, S40, S43, S46, S49, S52, S63, A8
January	S12, S21, S28, S47, S56, S70, S82, A9
February	S9, S18, S29, S32, S45, S48, S76, S83, A10, A11
March	S4, S17, S38, S41, S44, S60, A12, A13
April	S14, S24, S25, S39, S57, S68, S73, S74, A14
May	S5, S7, S22, S33, S42, S53, S67, S71, A15, A16
June	S8, S11, S34, S50, S55, S59, S72, A17
July	S3, S6, S15, S35, S61, S66, S74, A18, A19

Calendar of interesting dates

January

3   Birth of Father Damien in 1840. Could be linked with a 'Duty' theme and include Bible ref.: Mark 12: 13–17 and Colossians 3: 18–25. For more details of his life see 'Stories of Courage', by C. Mackinnon, pub. OUP. A useful address is: Leprosy Mission, 7 Bloomsbury Square, London WC1.
4   Birth of Louis Braille, 1909. Useful address: Royal National Institute for the Blind, 224-8 Great Portland Street, London W1.
6   Twelfth Night – celebration of the Three Wise Men visiting Jesus.
9   Funeral of Nelson, 1806.
14 Albert Schweitzer born, 1875. Bible ref.: Mark 2: 1–12.
24 Baden-Powell founded Boy Scouts, 1908.
25 Conversion of St Paul. Bible ref.: Acts 9: 1–31.
29 Origin of Victoria Cross 1856. Made from metal of guns captured in Crimea.

Last Tuesday in January – ceremonies recalling the ancient Viking tradition of sending dead chiefs to Valhalla in a blazing ship.

February

2   Candlemas. Festival of Jesus' presentation in the Temple of Jerusalem.
Cradle-rocking ceremonies of Middle Ages re-enacted the above. Village children were rocked in a wooden cradle before the altar whilst the *Nunc Dimitis* was being said. Bible ref.: Luke 2: 29.

5   Sir Robert Peel born, 1788. As founder of police this provides a link with 'people who help us'.

7   Charles Dickens born, 1812.

14   St Valentine's Day. Patron saint of birds. One Valentine was a priest who lived in Rome. Executed by Roman Emperor for sheltering Christians. Nineteenth century 'penny post' increased sending of Valentine cards. Early examples made of ribbons, lace, silk.

Shrovetide. The last three or four days before Lent were a time of feasting and revelry. Activities included hiding gates, removing door knockers, cock fighting, wrestling and practical jokes. Collop Monday saw the eating of large fried collops of meat; Shrove Tuesday, 'pancake day', was when eggs, fats and butter were used up in the making of pancakes. Ash Wednesday is the solemn beginning of Lent. Ashes were sprinkled on members of Church congregations to remind them of their mortality. For a Bible reference on Lent, Luke 4 is useful.

March

1   St David's Day. Patron saint of Wales, supposedly a great orator. Bible ref. in this connection James 3: 1–8.

3   Alexander Graham Bell born, 1847. Invented telephone. Useful for 'Communications' theme and for his work with deaf mutes.

17   St Patrick's Day. Kidnapped by pirates, about AD 400, and taken to Ireland. Later preached there. Patron saint of that country.

19   David Livingstone born, 1813. 'Missionary' Bible ref.: John 19: 17–27.

Lifeboat Day is in March. Interesting possibilities here. A useful address is: Royal National Lifeboat Institution, 42 Grosvenor Gardens, London SW1.

Mothering Sunday is fourth Sunday in Lent – traditionally a time when apprentices were allowed leave to visit their mothers.

Passion Sunday follows Mothering Sunday, it begins Passiontide and is remembered for Christ's suffering in the Garden of Gethsemane.

Palm Sunday celebrates Christ's entry into Jerusalem.

Easter eggs symbolise the Christian belief in renewal. A 'Spring' link is possible here with older, pagan beliefs being examined too.

Bible refs. for Easter could include: Mark 16: 1–8; Luke 23: 32–49. Of interest to children are details of the simnel cake – boiled then baked to settle the differences of the cooks.

April

1. All Fools' Day. One suggestion is that this was originally a sort of Jester National Holiday. As a result, whilst jesters were resting the rest of the population took the opportunity to play their tricks and have fun. Another suggestion is that it reflects Noah's foolishness in sending out a dove before the waters surrounding the ark had abated. This 'fool's errand' is also perpetuated in the legend of Demeter seeking her daughter Persephone who had been stolen away by the King of the Underworld.
2. Birth of Hans Anderson in 1805. The 'Ugly Duckling', an obvious possibility for assembly, is supposed to be autobiographical.
10. Birth of William Booth in 1829. Founder of the Salvation Army. Useful address: Salvation Army, 113 Queen Victoria Street, London EC4.
12. Yuri Gagarin. First man in space in 1961.
15. SS *Titanic* sank in 1912.
23. St George's Day. Patron saint of England and also soldiers and sailors. Supposedly a Roman army officer, ultimately beheaded for his Christian beliefs. Parades take place on Sunday nearest to St George's Day. Queen's Scouts parade through Windsor to a service in St George's Chapel.
Death of William Shakespeare in 1616.
25. St Mark's Day. Mark is supposed to have been an evangelist in the Middle East. Patron saint of Venice, his emblem is a lion.
28. Lord Shaftsbury born in 1801. Children find him an interesting subject and I have seen a good assembly based on an 'interview with Lord Shaftsbury'. There is a useful 'Jackdaw' on him.

Something could be made out of seasonal anecdotes like the one about the girl hearing the first cuckoo of the year. The number of times she hears the call is supposed to indicate the number of years she must wait before marriage.

May

1. Traditions for 1 May abound – crowning of the May Queen; traditional dances round the Maypole; parade of the 'hobby horses'; fairs and recreations of old English heroes like Robin Hood etc. One interesting custom to follow up was the tale that all village girls got up at dawn to wash their faces in dew to make sure they looked their

best. In some areas the eve of May Day was celebrated as 'Mischief Night'.
6 Roger Bannister became the first man to run a mile in four minutes, 1954.
12 Florence Nightingale born 1820. Useful Bible ref.: Psalm 46.
21 Elizabeth Fry born in 1750.
25 The new cathedral at Coventry consecrated in 1962.
26 St Augustine's Day. Augustine was the leader of a party of monks sent by Pope Gregory to bring Christianity to England. He landed in 597 and Canterbury Cathedral stands on the site of the monastery he established.
29 Conquest of Everest. The story of Hunt, Hillary and Tensing is told simply but well in *Great Men and Women of Modern Times*, pub. Purnell.

Oak Apple Day. The restoration of the monarchy was completed when Charles II entered Whitehall on this date in 1660. Celebrations took place throughout the country, but people were probably also remembering the king's escape by hiding in the famous oak tree after the Battle of Worcester. This occurred in September, 1651.

The three days before Ascension Day are Rogation Days. These were the days of prayer for a good harvest.

The celebration of Whitsuntide was a popular time for Miracle and Mystery plays. The latter were based on Biblical events. They are still featured in places like York, Chester and Coventry.

Whit Monday is still celebrated at local events like fairs. There is cheese-rolling in Gloucestershire, and one interesting anecdote for assembly is the Dunmow Flitch trial. The famous bacon flitch is awarded to the couple proving to have been the most happily married for a year and a day. Much has been written about this and there was even a film based on it. The chair in which the winners were carried through the streets can be seen in Little Dunmow church.

'Beating the Bounds' was another tradition associated with May. In the absence of maps the priest reminded his parishioners of the boundaries of the village by this practice.

June

June derives its name from Juno, the Roman goddess of marriage. It is traditionally a month for weddings. It is also associated with roses and there are some useful stories to follow up in connection with this flower.
1 Queen Elizabeth II was crowned in 1953.
6 Captain Scott was born in 1868 (refer again to *Great Men and Women of Modern Times*).

20 Queen Victoria's reign began in 1847.
22 St Alban – first English martyr.
24 John the Baptist Day. At Magdalen College, Oxford, a sermon is preached on the site where the hospital of John the Baptist once stood. Useful Bible refs. here are: Mark 6, for the story of the plot which cost John his life; Matthew 3, for his early days.
27 Helen Keller born 1880 (for useful address see 'Louis Braille' in January).
29 St Peter's Day. Chief of the twelve apostles. Is said to have become Bishop of Rome, and counts as the first pope, thus earning the true meaning of his name – 'Rock'. Many Biblical references in the Gospels and Acts.

June also sees Midsummer celebrations and there are connections with Stonehenge. 23 June was supposedly when spirits, witches, fairies etc. roamed at will. Huge bonfires were lit on Midsummer's Day. These had a twofold purpose: (*a*) to 'encourage' the sun to shine; (*b*) to keep away evil spirits. Young people often leapt through the bonfire flames, and livestock was often forced through them. This was in keeping with the superstition that such behaviour would result in a trouble-free year ahead.

July

4 United States Independence Day, 1776.
15 St Swithin's Day (died 862). St Swithin was a well-loved Bishop of Winchester who, by his own request, was buried in a humble manner. Some years later some monks sought to remove his grave to more elaborate surroundings in the cathedral. A tremendous rainstorm – supposedly lasting for forty days – stopped them so they took this to be a sign from God to leave the grave in peace. A useful related Bible ref. is: Genesis 6, 7 and 8.
21 In 1588 the battle with the Spanish Armada began on this day.
25 St Christopher's Day. The patron saint of travellers is symbolised by a palm-tree staff. A third-century saint, he was supposed to have carried a child of ever-increasing weight across a river. The child eventually proved to be Christ.
28 Hans Anderson died in 1875.
29 William Wilberforce died in 1833.

Other useful talking points and possible assembly ideas could stem from the fact that it was the most lethal month of all in the Great Plague of 1665. It is also the month associated with Rush Bearing, a very practical early tradition. As there were not even seats in most churches prior to the fifteenth century it was necessary to keep the earthen floor as dry as possible – hence the spreading of rushes on the floor. Rush bearing festivals still persist in one or two parts of the country.

August

1. This was traditionally the very earliest day associated with the Harvest Festival. Loaves of bread were taken to church to be consecrated (Lammas Day), and a traditional present of gloves was given to workers by their employers. This was to remind them of the hard harvesting ahead and also to protect their hands.
   Abolition of slavery in the British Empire in 1833. This was the work of William Wilberforce. A useful Bible ref. here would be Isaiah 35: 1–10.
6. Dropping of atom bomb on Hiroshima in 1945. For a Bible ref. denoting catastrophe and suffering: Job 1: 13–22.
13. John Logie Baird (inventor of television) born 1888.
24. St Bartholomew's Day. Patron saint of bees and honey. Link with the ceremonial drinking of mead – once thought to keep a marriage contented and fruitful.

The first week in August sees the occasion of the Royal National Eisteddfodd in Wales, in which the inaugural ceremony includes the presentation of the Sword of Peace.

The last Sunday in August recalls one of the most moving stories of the Great Plague. A parcel of clothes was sent from London in 1665 to a tailor in a village called Eyam in Derbyshire. The clothes must have been contaminated, and caused a rapid spread of the disease in the village. The Rector persuaded the entire village to 'seal its boundaries' so the disease could not spread. Food was left on the outskirts and collected by fit villagers. Most of the population died but the infection did not spread. The event is commemorated in the village every year by an open air service.

September

2–6 Great Fire of London in 1666. This is a useful beginning for an assembly that could move on to a theme of 'Fire'.
15. Battle of Britain Day.
18. Birth of Samuel Johnson, 1709.
19. Death of Dr Barnardo in 1905.
21. St Matthew's Day. One of the twelve apostles, he is often identified with Levi, a former tax collector. Bible refs.: Mark 2; Luke 5, 6.
29. St Michael's Day. Supposedly the archangel who protected the Hebrew nation. Michaelmas offers many interesting follow-ups. There was the tradition of delaying the payment of rents by making presents of geese to landlords. Queen Elizabeth I was said to have been eating goose when news was brought to her of the defeat of the Armada on 29 September 1588. To make a convenient nautical link here, Nelson was born on this date in 1758.

September has always been one of the months associated with harvest. The ceremony of decorating the last sheaf of corn in the field is a pre-Christian link with the Roman goddess Ceres. Reference also might be made to Michaelmas daisies which are still much in evidence for the decorating of churches at harvest festivals. The Rev. R.S. Hawker, Vicar of Morwenstow in Cornwall, was credited with holding the first harvest festival service in 1843.

October

3 Feast of St Francis.
6 Death of William Tyndale, translator of the Bible into English, who was executed in 1536. Useful starting point for work on Bibles. Helpful address here is: British and Foreign Bible Society, 146 Queen Victoria Street, London EC4.
10 Lord Nuffield born in 1877. Useful for work on generosity, rich giving to poor etc. An interesting anecdote is the one about Lord Nuffield giving a poppy seller a cheque for £100,000 on Remembrance Day.
12 Discovery of America by Columbus in 1492.
14 Battle of Hastings, 1066.
15 Gladys Aylward left for missionary work in China in 1932.
18 St Luke's Day. Author of the third gospel and a friend of St Paul.
21 Trafalgar Day, 1805. Many thematic possibilities here, ranging from 'Courage', 'The sea' to 'Peace'.
24 United Nations Day.
31 All Hallows' Eve. Traditionally one of the most significant days of the calendar. As the night went all the harvest had to be gathered in before the onset of winter, it was held with a mixture of sadness, celebration and relief. Fear was present because of its associations with the revels of witches and evil spirits. The traditions of Hallowe'en are numerous – for more information please note the books recommended in the 'Special Occasions' section of 'Resources' (p.155).

The 'Harvest' theme of October is an important one for assembly considerations. Consequently, useful Bible refs. could include: Matthew 13:3; Luke 8 for the story of the sower; Ruth 1–4 for the story of Ruth and Boaz.

Appropriate music could range from Beethoven's Pastoral Symphony (No. 6 – 3rd Movement) to 'Joseph and the Amazing Technicoloured Dreamcoat', Decca SKL 4973. Poems might include ones like Keats' 'Autumn', Laurie Lee's 'Apples', Seamus Heaney's 'Blackberry Picking', and Peter Mullineaux's 'Harvest Festival'.

One final seasonal anecdote can lead to some interesting dramatic possibilites for assembly. Traditionally, October was a time for job-changing. At the many fairs up and down the country job seekers stood in the market place waiting and hoping for someone to offer them work.

November

1   All Saints' Day. The day when saints without a special 'day' of their own are remembered in the Church calendar.
5   Florence Nightingale began her work in Scutari in 1855.
    Guy Fawkes Night, 1604. Much can be made of this for assembly. One strong possibility is a comparative link with the Hindu festival of Diwali. There are strong common factors running through both of these occasions and their dates are often close to each other. On November 5 1972, for example, they were actually on the same date.
11 St Martin's Day. A useful alternative to the 'Good Samaritan'. Martin was a Roman soldier in France. The story is that he gave half of his cloak to a beggar. As a result of a dream afterwards he became a Christian and later a monk.

    Remembrance Day is a time when old newspapers are very useful for an assembly presentation connected with memories. They can form a useful contribution to the preparatory work for a class assembly which could be given either just before or just after Remembrance Sunday. This is an assembly theme that could use visual impact very strongly. The hall itself and the approaches to it could contain mobile displays based on a 'Do you remember' theme. Along with newspapers, excerpts from school logbooks could be reproduced, as could photographs of last year's sports day, portraits of the recent scholars and so on.
30 St Andrew's Day. Apostle and brother of Simon Peter. Patron Saint of Scotland. His grave is supposed to be at St Andrews in Scotland. Preached in Middle East and Russia, also patron saint of Russia.

The second Saturday in November is the day of the Lord Mayor's Show in London.

A useful poem to have on hand this month is Thomas Hood's 'November'.

December

4   Edith Cavell born in 1865 (ref. *Great Men and Women of Modern Times* again).
6   St Nicholas' Day. Patron saint of children, though there are more celebrations of this day on the continent than in England. Children

have their shoes filled with sweets in some countries. Ancient tradition of enthroning a 'temporary Boy Bishop' is still carried out in some places. In this ceremony a boy (usually a chorister these days) is allowed to wear the vestments of a Bishop.

13   St Lucy's (Lucia) Day.
17   First flight of Wright brothers in 1903.

Information and traditions surrounding Christmas are too numerous for other than a brief mention here. Christmas decorations are certainly pre-Christian and signified life and promise in the middle of winter; berries on the holly can be symbolic of the blood Christ shed for man; mistletoe is the symbol of love in the ancient story of Baldur, who was killed by a sprig of mistletoe but then brought back to life by the Norse gods, who made a promise that mistletoe would never hurt again; Christmas boxes are linked to the old opening and giving from the parish poor box; Christmas trees were brought from Germany by Queen Victoria's husband Prince Albert; mince pies go back to the times when Crusaders first brought spices from the Holy Land; many ancient mumming plays were performed at Christmas, the theme being 'Good' defeats 'Evil'; many carols originate from the nineteenth century, others from as long ago as the thirteenth century; Christmas cards originated just over a hundred years ago.

Biblical refs. for the Nativity story are: Luke 2: 1–20; Matthew 2: 1–12.

'Inspiring lives' (grouped under relevant themes)

Courage

St Stephen, first martyr; St Alban, first English martyr; Joan of Arc.
Leonidas of Sparta; David (v Goliath) – physical courage.
Douglas Bader and James Wolf – courage conquering personal difficulties, as well as a country's enemies at war.
Charles Lindburgh and Amy Johnson – courage in achieving 'firsts'.
Bishop Bergrav of Norway – courage of one's convictions (against Nazis in Second World War).
Beethoven – courage to persevere despite specific physical handicap.

Unselfishness

Father Damien – helped lepers; Dr Barnardo; Albert Schweitzer – hospital at Lamberene; Gladys Aylward.
Lawrence Oates – Scott's Antarctic expedition.
Martin Luther King – negro minister who was assassinated whilst seeking to further the cause of underprivileged negroes.

Alan Paton – opponent of apartheid.
Trevor Huddleston – opponent of apartheid and campaigner for reform to help London's underprivileged.

Spirit of service/sense of duty

Florence Nightingale.
St Lucia – Festival of Light commemorates her aid to Christians in hiding.
Nathaniel Saint – pilot/missionary in Equador.
William Carey – work in India.
John Ashley – founder of 'Missions to Seamen'.
Kwegir Aggrey – African educationist, famous for his reference to the piano keyboard in symbolic vein: 'For harmony you must use both black and white.'
Andrew Carnegie – on becoming a millionaire gave away huge sums to help others, particularly remembered for gifts to libraries.
John Wesley – 'I look upon the world as my parish.'
William Booth – founder of the Salvation Army.
Lord Shaftsbury – saviour of working children.
Baden Powell – founder of Scouts (1908) and Guides (1910).
William Tyndale – first English Bible.
Mother Theresa – cares for incurables abandoned on streets of Calcutta, Nobel prize winner.
Chad Varah – founder of the 'Samaritans'.
Henry Dunant – founder of the Red Cross.
Father Borelli – social worker in the slums of Naples.
Elizabeth Garrett – first English woman doctor.
Bishop Fleming – work with Eskimos.
Elizabeth Fry – social reform in women's prisons.
Edith Cavell – nurse who helped wounded soldiers in enemy territory.
Alexander Graham Bell – invented telephone and also did much work to help educate deaf mutes.
William Wilberforce – abolition of slavery.
Grace Darling – lifeboat heroine.
Toyohiko Kagawa – Japanese Christian, aided unions, unemployed, housing reform.
Mahatma Gandhi – protest through non-violence.

Resources

The resources for Music and Assembly, and Assemblies and Religions, have already been given in the appropriate sections of this book. This resource section is therefore divided into the following categories:
1 'Assembly' books containing material and suggestions.
2 Books containing a wide selection of suitable stories.
3 Poetry anthologies.
4 Books for teacher reference.
5 Magazines.
6 Material for special occasions in assembly.
7 The best Bibles, and related books, for this age-group.
8 Books containing drama suggestions for assembly.
9 Anthologies of prayers.
10 Audio-visual material.

1 Assembly books containing material and suggestions

A Book of Assemblies, by Derek Waters, pub. Mills and Boon. This is a book of suggestions rather than 'instant' assemblies. It contains much that will aid good practice.

Primary School Assemblies – Stories and Ideas, by Frank Pinfold, pub. Ward Lock Educational. A good selection of 'fresh' stories with appropriate suggestions for development.

Assembly: Poems and Prose, collected by Redvers Brandling, pub. Macmillan. This anthology of poems and prose links both thematically with a wide variety of subjects suitable for assembly.

Primary School Assembly Book, by F. Dickinson and I.R. Worsnop, pub. Macmillan. A good book for wide ranging information and assembly ideas.

Day by Day, by Rowland Purton, pub. Basil Blackwell. A detailed compilation that seeks to provide 'stories and prayers for every day of the year'.

Assembly Workshop, compiled and edited by Ronald Dingwall, pub. Darton, Longman and Todd. This file contains much that is useful for assembly and its detailed cross references are valuable for building up varied presentations.

Celebrating Together – A Resource Book for Primary Assemblies, by Peter Wetz and Pauline Walker, pub. Darton, Longman and Todd. This is another file full of most useful ideas and information.

2 Books containing a wide selection of suitable stories

Pause for Thought – 25 stories for Assembly, by Molly Cheston, pub. Blackie.

101 Assembly Stories, by Frank Carr, pub. Foulsham. This is a varied selection of stories, all beautifully told, and ready for 'instant' use.

Further Stories for the Junior Assembly, edited by Dorothy M. Prescott, pub. Blanford Press.

Stories for the 8–11s, compiled by Paul Morton-George, pub. Denholm House Press.

Tell me a story, chosen by Eileen Colwell, pub. Puffin.

Stories for seven year olds, edited by Sara and Stephen Corrin, pub. Puffin.

The Anita Hewitt Animal Story Book, pub. Puffin.

The three books above yield plenty of stories for children at the bottom end of the primary school. They are useful for guiding young children's attention to the world around them

The Goalkeeper's Revenge, by Bill Naughton, pub. Puffin.
My Pal Spadger, by Bill Naughton, pub. Dent Dolphin.
Islands in the Sky, by Arthur C. Clarke, pub. Puffin.
These three books provide many suitable and thought-provoking stories for use with children in the top part of the primary school.

There are also many children's novels available which provide excellent passages for assembly purposes. These passages could be read aloud, once the right context has been established, and many would be useful for dramatic presentation. The following books might be used in this way:
I am David, by Anne Holm, pub. Puffin Macmillan M. Books
Carrie's War, by Nina Bawden, pub. Puffin.
The House of Sixty Fathers, by Meindert De Jong, pub. Puffin.
The Dolphin Crossing, by Jill Paton Walsh, pub. Puffin.
The Tenth Good Thing about Barney, by Judith Viorst, pub. Collins.
A Fair Few Days, by Jane Gardam, pub. Puffin.

Four useful books of true stories which could be used for assemblies are:
Stories of Courage, by George MacKinnon, pub. OUP.
Great Leaders, by Cleodie MacKinnon, pub. OUP.
Great Leaders, by R.J. Unstead, pub. Carousel.
Piccolo Book of Heroines, by Richard Garrett, pub. Pan.

3 Poetry anthologies

My World: poems from Living Language, edited by Joan Griffiths, pub. the BBC. A tasteful collection covering areas such as: a day at school; playing out; street; home time; a world an inch away from ours; others; that's me.
Thoughtshapes, Bandstand, Bandwagon. These three are all by Barry Maybury, pub. OUP. Themes include people; reflections; story; machines; everyday things; natural things.
Complete poems for children, by James Reeves, pub. Heinemann. A selection of poems incorporating both sad and happy occasions.
Junior Voices, Bks. 1, 2, 3 and 4, edited by G. Summerfield, pub. Penguin. A collection of evocative poems illustrated by some good pictures.
Drums and Trumpets, selected by Leonard Clark, pub. Bodley Head. These are poems for young children taking their first look at the world around them – seasons, living things etc.
Who am I?, by Margaret Greaves, pub. Methuen Educational. This is a collection of poems related to thoughts and words concerning personal experiences.

Poems for the School Assembly and Other Occasions, edited by Dorothy M. Prescott, pub. Blandford Press.

Say it Aloud, a selection of poems edited for the Poetry Society by Norman Hidden, pub. Hutchinson. These two volumes contain a wide range of poems most useful for assembly, many written by children themselves.

4 Books for teacher reference

Behold the Land: A Pictorial Atlas of the Bible, by F.H. Hilliard, pub. George Philip.

Everyday Life in Old Testament Times, by E.W. Heaton, pub. Carousel. Contains some excellent, simple maps that are very easily re-drawn.

Signs and Symbols in Christian Art, by George Ferguson, pub. OUP. This is a fascinating book packed with an enormous amount of incidental detail that is very useful for a wide range of assemblies.

What do you think?, by David and Christina Millman, pub. Blackie. A stimulating little book that provokes many assembly ideas – and material to support them.

World Religions, by F.G. Herod, pub. Blond Educational. Succinct information and excellent photographs.

On Location – Churches, by Henry Pluckrose, pub. Mills and Boon.

First School RE – a guide for Teachers, by Terence and Gill Cropley, pub. SCM Press Ltd.

5 Magazines

The Christian Education Movement (2 Chester House, Pages Lane, London NW10 1PR) regularly produces magazine-type publications that are extremely valuable in connection with primary school assemblies and RE in general. To give just some examples of the subjects they have covered: 'Festivals' (Primary Mailing No. 10); 'Symbols' (Primary Mailing No. 12); 'Religious Education and the Multi-Cultural Society' (Primary Resource Vol. 5, No. 3); 'The Bible' (Special Supplement – Christianity 3).

Together, edited by Pamela Egan and published by the Church Information Office (Church House, Dean's Yard, London SW1) is an excellent little monthly magazine. If often contains detailed ideas for assemblies.

From time to time Christian Aid (PO Box No. 1, London SW1W 9BW) publishes in magazine format suggestions for junior and infant assemblies. These are well thought-out, detailed and excellently produced. Queries about them should be directed to Christian Aid.

6 Material for special occasions in assembly

Days of the Year, by Joyce McLellan, pub. Religious Education Press. A small book with information about St Patrick's Day, St George's Day, Easter Day etc.

Festive Occasions in the Primary School, by Redvers Brandling, pub. Ward Lock Educational. The 'occasions' are Harvest, Hallowe'en, 5 November, Christmas, 14 February, 1 April, Easter, 1 May, Midsummer, St Swithin's, and some from other cultures. There are assemblies described for each occasion.

Celebrations, by Derek Waters, pub. Mills and Boon. Includes celebrations of May, Flowers, the Street, Good neighbours etc.

Christmas in the Primary School, by Redvers Brandling, pub. Ward Lock Educational. Contains much material that would be useful for Christmas assemblies and presentation.

Festivals, compiled by Ruth Manning-Sanders, pub. Heinemann. The subject here is festivals from all over the world. The arrangement allows them to be presented month by month.

Together for Harvest, *Together for Christmas*, *Together for Festivals*, *Together again for Christmas* – all published by the Church Information Office, all with good assembly ideas.

7 The best Bibles, and related books, for this age-group

The New English Bible, pub. OUP and CUP.

Winding Quest – the Heart of the Old Testament in Plain English, by Alan T. Dale, pub. OUP.

New World – the Heart of the New Testament in Plain English, by Alan T. Dale, pub. OUP.

The New Testament in Modern English, by J.B. Phillips, pub. Collins.

These four books would be an asset to any school; in fact they could almost be called essentials for a satisfactory RE/Assembly programme.

The Bible Data Book, by N. Bull, pub. Evans.

The Book of the Bible – an encyclopedic guide to the World's Greatest Book, edited by John Grisewood, pub. Purnell. This has readable, informative text and excellent illustrations and photographs.

The New Black's Bible Dictionary, by Madeleine S. and J. Lane Miller, pub. A. and C. Black. This is very useful for teacher reference.

8 Books containing drama suggestions

Plays for Assembly, by Peter M. Allen, pub. Schofield and Sims. These plays lean heavily on a narrator, but the book is good value with fifty-five little dramas to choose from.
Dramatic Worship for the School Assembly, by Peter A. White, pub. Religious Education Press. Ten prepared plays for direct use.
Miracle Man, a folk musical by Pamela Verrall (whose music always seems to go down well with Juniors), pub. Kevin Mayhew Ltd. This play has spoken and sung parts and would be most suitable for Easter.
Radio Jerusalem, by Charles J. Kitchel, pub. Ginn. Some useful examples of 'radio type' drama here.

9 Anthologies of prayers

The National Christian Education Council, Denholm House Press, have published three useful paperback books in a 'Prayers' series. These are: *Prayers to use with 5–8s, Prayers to use with 8–11s, Prayers to use with 11–13s.*
In Excelsis, by H.W. Dobson, pub. Church Information Office. This is a collection intended for children of junior school age.
Contemporary prayers for Church and School, edited by Caryl Micklem, pub. SCM Press.
Well God, here we are again, by John Byrant and David Winter, pub. Hodder and Stoughton. Some original prayers in this book in 'the everyday language of children themselves'.
Treat Me Cool, Lord, by Carl Burke, pub. Collins Fontana. American, adult and humorous, this paperback nevertheless offers some stimulating material, which can be modified for use with children.

10 Audio-visual material

Audio

'Sea, Clouds and Rain', a cassette containing two ten-minute programmes on poems, stories, songs and Bible dramas (for 6–8 year-olds) with a teacher's booklet. It is available on SU C4 from Scripture Union (47 Marylebone Lane, London W1M 6AX).
'Two stories Jesus told' read by Derek Nimmo, available from Scripture

Union/Ladybird. This is a cassette of Derek Nimmo reading the Ladybird book versions of the Prodigal Son and the Good Samaritan.
'Watch, Look, Listen', Fisherfolk Kit 2, available from Celebration Services (Dept. T1, 57 Dorchester Road, Lytchett Minster, Poole, Dorset, BH16 6JE). This is a cassette selection of readings, drama and music, particularly appropriate to Christmas. Other useful selections of the Fisherfolk's work can also be obtained from the same address.

Visual

'Nature during the four seasons' – slide folio available from The Slide Centre (Portman House, 17 Broderick Road, London SW17 7DZ).
A set of colour posters related to homes and families is available from Christian Education Movement (see address under 'Magazines').
'Portrait of Jesus' BBC Radio Vision Filmstrip.
'Everyday life in Palestine', Film strip No. FF79 from Concordia.
'The Child Jesus' and 'In the Beginning' are two packs of sixteen colour slides each, which are available in the Ladybird Bible Slide Pack Series.
'New Testament Pictures for Today', 'New Testament Pictures for Today' (second series), 'Old Testament Pictures for Today'. These are all published by the Church Information Office and have helpful accompanying leaflets (in the case of the latter, written by Alan Dale).
'The People of this World belong Together', pub. National Christian Education Council, Denholm House Press. Twenty coloured slides of pictures painted by children, commissioned by the World Council of Churches. There is a commentary handbook. Most useful for a 'whole school' assembly of infants and juniors.